ANNE
FRANK

ANNE
FRANK

Other titles in the
People Who Made History series:

ANNE FRANK

Jennifer Hansen, *Book Editor*

Daniel Leone, *President*
Bonnie Szumski, *Publisher*
Scott Barbour, *Managing Editor*
David M. Haugen, *Series Editor*

GREENHAVEN
PRESS®

San Diego • Detroit • New York • San Francisco • Cleveland
New Haven, Conn. • Waterville, Maine • London • Munich

THOMSON

GALE

LIBRARY OF CONGRESS CATALOGING-IN-PUBLICATION DATA

Anne Frank / Jennifer Hansen, book editor.
  p. cm. — (People who made history)
Includes bibliographical references and index.
ISBN 0-7377-1708-4 (pbk. : alk. paper) — ISBN 0-7377-1707-6 (lib. : alk. paper)
  1. Frank, Anne, 1929–1945. 2. Jews—Netherlands—Amsterdam—Biography.
3. Jewish children in the Holocaust—Netherlands—Amsterdam—Biography.
4. Jewish girls—Netherlands—Amsterdam—Biography. 5. Holocaust, Jewish
(1939–1945)—Netherlands—Amsterdam—Personal narratives—History and
criticism. 6. Jews—Persecutions—Netherlands—Amsterdam. 7. Frank, Anne,
1929–1945. Achterhuis. I. Hansen, Jennifer.
DS135.N6 F7316 2003
940.53'18'092—dc21   2002035427
  [B]

1/06   B+T   2370 /2370

CONTENTS

all the classic stages of development, including how she related to parents, boys, and growing up.

Chapter 2: Arrest and Annihilation

Chapter 3: Anne Frank, the Writer

Chapter 4: Anne Frank's Legacy

FOREWORD

In the vast and colorful pageant of human history, a handful of individuals stand out. They are the men and women who have come variously to be called "great," "leading," "brilliant," "pivotal," or "infamous" because they and their deeds forever changed their own society or the world as a whole. Some were political or military leaders—kings, queens, presidents, generals, and the like—whose policies, conquests, or innovations reshaped the maps and futures of countries and entire continents. Among those falling into this category were the formidable Roman statesman/general Julius Caesar, who extended Rome's power into Gaul (what is now France); Caesar's lover and ally, the notorious Egyptian queen Cleopatra, who challenged the strongest male rulers of her day; and England's stalwart Queen Elizabeth I, whose defeat of the mighty Spanish Armada saved England from subjugation.

Some of history's other movers and shakers were scientists or other thinkers whose ideas and discoveries altered the way people conduct their everyday lives or view themselves and their place in nature. The electric light and other remarkable inventions of Thomas Edison, for example, revolutionized almost every aspect of home-life and the workplace; and the theories of naturalist Charles Darwin lit the way for biologists and other scientists in their ongoing efforts to understand the origins of living things, including human beings.

Still other people who made history were religious leaders and social reformers. The struggles of the Arabic prophet Muhammad more than a thousand years ago led to the establishment of one of the world's great religions—Islam; and the efforts and personal sacrifices of an American reverend named Martin Luther King Jr. brought about major improvements in race relations and the justice system in the United States.

Each anthology in the People Who Made History series begins with an introductory essay that provides a general overview of the individual's life, times, and contributions. The group of essays that follow are chosen for their accessibility to a young adult audience and carefully edited in consideration of the reading and comprehension levels of that audience. Some of the essays are by noted historians, professors, and other experts. Others are excerpts from contemporary writings by or about the pivotal individual in question. To aid the reader in choosing the material of immediate interest or need, an annotated table of contents summarizes the article's main themes and insights.

Each volume also contains extensive research tools, including a collection of excerpts from primary source documents pertaining to the individual under discussion. The volumes are rounded out with an extensive bibliography and a comprehensive index.

Plutarch, the renowned first-century Greek biographer and moralist, crystallized the idea behind Greenhaven's People Who Made History when he said, "To be ignorant of the lives of the most celebrated men of past ages is to continue in a state of childhood all our days." Indeed, since it is people who make history, every modern nation, organization, institution, invention, artifact, and idea is the result of the diligent efforts of one or more individuals, living or dead; and it is therefore impossible to understand how the world we live in came to be without examining the contributions of these individuals.

INTRODUCTION: ANNE FRANK: "SIMPLY A YOUNG GIRL"

Each year, school children in many nations read and study a diary that was written by someone their own age. Though she died over fifty years ago, this one young girl's life has made a lasting impact on the world. Her diary, her legacy, bears witness to a turbulent and horrific period in history, as well as to the single life of an otherwise average teenager. Was Anne Frank really, as she writes in her diary, "simply a young girl"? Or was she an extraordinary one? Though she died at the young age of fifteen, Anne is celebrated throughout the world as people read her diary, watch the play or movie based on her life, or visit the traveling museum exhibit that documents her life. The attraction is apparent, but the life behind the story is anything but simple.

ANNE'S BEGINNING

Born on June 12, 1929, Anneliese Marie's early years were quite ordinary. Her parents, Otto and Edith Hollander Frank, were an older couple. Anne had a sister, Margot, who was three years old when Anne was born. They lived in a charming community in the German town of Frankfurt am Maim, where Otto ran a successful business, producing pectin to make jam.

Though Jewish by birth, the Franks were Germans first and foremost. Edith Frank was religious and went to synagogue and celebrated the Jewish holidays throughout her life. Her husband Otto, however, was an assimilated Jew. Though he was born a Jew, he was not religious. Otto wanted only to fit into the German community and even fought for Germany in World War I. For Anne, still a young girl, being raised by a practicing Jewish mother and an assimilated Jewish father led to having a sense of tradition coupled with a desire to blend in. Unfortunately, by 1932 when the Nazis were elected to positions of power in Germany, it mattered only if you were a Jew—whether practicing or not.

THE FLIGHT TO AMSTERDAM

The Frank family realized that being Jewish was going to cause them trouble in a Nazi-controlled nation. Upon losing World War I, Germany was stripped of much of its prestige and power. The Treaty of Versailles, which officially ended the war, forced the Germans to accept blame for the entire war, which made many German citizens angry. At the same time, the world was experiencing economic depression, which caused the German people to lose even more hope. Into this climate of despair and anger, the Nazi—or National Socialist German Workers' Party—was created. When it was founded in 1920, it was considered a radical group. The party wanted to ignore the Treaty of Versailles and give the German people back their pride.

From the very beginning the Nazi Party was anti-Semitic. Looking for someone to blame for Germany's defeat in the war, Adolf Hitler—the mastermind behind Nazi ideology— singled out the Jews. Since many Germans were tired of living under the shadow of past defeat and economic ruin, they were eager to accept Hitler's explanation that the Jews had undermined Germany's pride and martial strength.

Thus, when Nazi Party members were elected to a majority of the government positions in 1932, they had the backing of the citizens of Germany, and they began to create laws placing severe restrictions on the Jews. In an attempt to boost the German economy and cripple "Jewish influence" in the nation, the Nazis created and enacted laws throughout Germany that made it impossible for Jews to run businesses. First Jewish businesses were boycotted, then books by Jewish authors were banned, then more and more restrictions were placed on the daily activities of Jewish citizens. Although few people may have realized it at the time, Adolf Hitler's grand plan was to eliminate all the Jews in Europe. The laws and boycotts against the Jews simply ushered in the beginning of the Holocaust, the genocide of European Jewry.

During the summer of 1933 Otto Frank decided to flee Germany and the oppressive anti-Semitic policies. He moved his immediate family—Edith, Margot, and little four-year-old Anne—to the city of Amsterdam in the Netherlands. There he created another company and continued to do business.

ANNE AS A CHILD

Throughout this trying time, Anne had a wonderful childhood. She and Margot were well loved, cared for, and surrounded by family and friends. Anne was spunky. When the family relocated to Amsterdam it was Anne who had no problems making new friends and helping the family integrate into a new community. There were many German refugees in Amsterdam at this time; they had emigrated to escape the dangers of Nazi Germany. Anne became friends with many other German children, all of whom learned the Dutch language quickly and fit in easier than their parents did.

Anne Frank

Many of Anne's friends remember her as the center of attention. Anne loved to watch movies and collect photos of movie stars. She was interested in the Dutch royal family. She loved to read. By all accounts, Anne was a normal child. And she was precocious, lively, and outspoken—perl   ery outspoken. Anne's best friend, Hanneli Goslar (who   ne calls Lies in her diary) fondly remembers one of   friends' mother saying, "God knows everything, but Anne knows everything better."[1] Even as a young girl Anne had strong opinions and often made snap judgments about people. Like many girls she changed friends quickly and laughed one moment and cried the next. Though she is well remembered by those who loved her, she was not especially gifted. She was simply Anne.

THE NAZIS TAKE OVER THE NETHERLANDS

In 1939 World War II began as German\   . Poland. All of Europe waited tensely for Hitler's ne   . He invaded western Europe, including the Nether .nds, in 1940. By the time Amsterdam was taken, Anne's life was no longer normal. As the Nazis imposed anti-Jewish laws on the conquered lands, Anne's family began to experience the very things that they had fled Germany to avoid: Jews could not ride trains, own bicycles, shop in general stores, or be outside after 8 P.M. They were forced to wear the yellow Star of

David to indicate that they were of Jewish descent.

As restrictions placed on the Jews grew more and more limiting, Anne's father secretly began to make plans for the entire family to go into hiding. The Nazis had already begun to force the Jews to move into ghettos and to send them to concentration camps, where most Jews were worked to death or killed in some other manner. Fearing for their lives, many Jewish families went to great measures to protect themselves from the Nazis. Those who were lucky found the means to leave Europe altogether. Others sent their children to live with relatives in countries, such as England or the United States, that were considered safe. Many families were split apart as one by one their members found places to hide. Those who couldn't escape or chose to remain were typically rounded up by the Nazi police. Some were sent to work camps, others to extermination camps. Unable to get his family out of Amsterdam, Otto Frank chose to hide them from the Nazis and wait out the war.

ANNE'S DIARY

During this time Anne lived under extraordinary circumstances that transformed her from "simply a young girl" into one who would be remembered for an extraordinary legacy. Anne turned thirteen only a few weeks before her family would "disappear of our own accord."[2] For her birthday Anne received a diary, and she began to write about her experiences. She decided to name her diary Kitty and treated it as a special friend—the kind of friend she had always wanted. In the weeks before she went into hiding the diary entries were typical of a thirteen-year-old. Anne wrote about what she studied in school, her friends, and what she thought about boys. As she wrote about the ordinary things in her life, the diary became more than just a day book to Anne. It was a place for her to write and explore herself: "I want to write, but more than that, I want to bring out all kinds of things that lie buried deep in my heart."[3] When her family fled their home on July 6, 1942, and took up residence hiding in a secret annex of the building that housed her father's business, the diary became so much more.

LIFE IN HIDING

Though Anne didn't know it, Otto Frank had been preparing for the family to go into hiding for a long time. When her sister Margot unexpectedly got a notice to attend work camp, the family decided to go into hiding the next day. Anne had less than twenty-four hours to prepare and pack her things. She wasn't able to tell anyone, not even her best friends. She wrote in her diary that the only creature she was allowed to say good-bye to was the cat she had to leave behind. The family walked from their house to her father's office building. The family had no idea how long they would have to live in hiding. With the help of Otto's business partners and staff who continued to work in Otto's office building, the family would spend twenty-five months secluded from the outside world.

In addition to the four members of the Frank family, Otto Frank's Jewish business partner, Hermann van Pels (whom Anne renames Van Daan in her diary), his wife, Auguste, and their son, Peter, joined them in hiding. Seven people (eventually eight, when a Jewish dentist, Fritz Pfeffer—whom Anne called Dussel—joined them) were forced to create a "normal" existence within the tight confines of the "Secret Annex," the name Anne gave to their hiding place. Hidden behind a bookcase in the offices of Otto Frank's company, Opekta, the annex was actually two floors of rooms with an attic. When they first arrived, Anne and Margot shared a small room that Anne decorated with photos of movie stars and the royal family. Upon the arrival of Pfeffer, Margot moved to a cot, and Anne had to share her room with the dentist.

Though it took some time to establish their space and routines, each member did just that. Even rambunctious Anne settled into a routine. Her father taught the three children in the annex. She would clean, do her schoolwork, and—most importantly—write in her diary. It was her diary that would keep Anne's spirits up for the twenty-five months that she lived there.

LIFE IN THE ANNEX

Life in the annex was often quite dull, particularly for a teenager as social and vivacious as Anne. Like any young writer, Anne wrote little about the mundane experiences of her life in hiding; instead, she focused on those times that were especially noteworthy. Though in many ways one day simply melted into another in the annex, Anne's diary reveals that she was able to make even those times into something worth reading and writing about.

Some days held special interest for Anne. Sometimes one

of Otto's business partners would come and be their guest for lunch or dinner, or simply bring news from the outside world. Miep Gies, one of the office workers who kept the family hidden, remembers visiting the annex: "And when my face appeared above the landing, all eyes would light upon me. A flash of enthusiasm would widen all eyes. . . . Then Anne, always Anne, would be upon me with a rapid-fire barrage of questions."[4] Interaction with the outside world renewed Anne's hope—and fueled her enthusiasm to write.

Even a day with no guests could merit special notice, usually because of the inevitable arguments that living so close together caused. "Every time I write to you something special seems to have happened but they are more often unpleasant than pleasant things,"[5] she confided to her diary. Anne wrote about the many quarrels that erupted between inhabitants of the annex, frequently as the result of something she herself had done. Anne's personality was so open and boisterous that it often got her into trouble with the adults in the annex, particularly her roommate and Mrs. van Pels. Following a disagreement with her mother, Anne wrote: "Dear Kitty, I'm boiling with rage, and yet I mustn't show it. I'd like to stamp my feet, scream, give Mummy a good shaking, cry, and I don't know what else, because of the horrible words, mocking looks, and accusations which are leveled at me repeatedly every day, and find their mark, like shafts from a tightly strung bow, and which are just as hard to draw from my body."[6]

THE "REAL" ANNE

Despite the fact that some of the people she lived with thought Anne was flighty and unconcerned with their opinion of her, she was very sensitive to criticism. Often she was her own harshest judge. "The whole day long I hear nothing else but that I am an insufferable baby, and although I laugh about it and pretend not to take any notice. I *do* mind. I would like to ask God to give me a different nature, so that I didn't put everyone's back up."[7]

Remembered as being outspoken and often the cause of disagreements and strife in the annex, Anne revealed several different sides of herself in her diary. Her writing displayed the personality of a normal teenage girl: Anne criticized those who lived with her, she was catty and mean to her sister and mother, and she often complained (to her diary, at least) that she didn't get enough of what she wanted. But she also wrote about her desire to grow and change, to become more of the person she dreamed she could become. Her sensitivity to what others thought of her forced her to look at herself more closely, and though she may have hidden her hurt feelings, she poured her emotions into her diary and "friend," Kitty.

A LIFE OF WRITING

Writing was a great comfort to this girl caught between childhood and adulthood while in the confines of hiding. She lived in fear for her life, yet at the same time was grateful for her present safety. Anne wanted to spend her time wisely so that she might someday be remembered: "I want to go on living even after my death."[8] Glimpses of the seriousness with which she wrote can be found in how she was perceived by the other members of the annex, as well as their protectors. Miep Gies remembers, "I saw that Anne was writing intently . . . I saw a look on her face at this moment that I'd never seen before. It was a look of dark concentration, as if she had a throbbing headache. This look pierced me, and I was speechless."[9]

Writing became Anne's means to living a full life. She may have been unable to go outside for over two years, talk during the day for fear of being found, or sleep without having to rest her feet on a chair, but she was able to develop and grow emotionally because of the time she spent with her written thoughts.

Anne Frank is remembered today because her words gave voice to a life few people have ever imagined, much less experienced. However, she really was "simply a young girl." Her original diary entries were often heated and without self-censorship. They reflected the whims, swinging emotions, and hotheaded words of a typical teenager trying to figure out who she was and what she wanted. However, just a few months before Anne's diary ended she heard a radio broadcast in which a member of the Dutch parliament stated that diaries and letters from the war would be collected for publication at war's end. This excited Anne greatly as it was a chance to begin her career as a famous writer.

Anne began to edit her diary with an eye toward this future publication, changing names, reworking different "scenes," and deleting passages that didn't please her. Suddenly, the diary was no longer simply a place to reveal her deepest thoughts and emotions. Though she continued to keep her diary as before, she was careful to consider a future readership when she edited sections she had previously written. For the first time she experienced the conflict of Anne the diarist and Anne the future author.

THE ARREST

Life in the annex, even with the comfort of her family and diary, was not easy. Anne wrote of lying in bed as Allied warplanes bombed Amsterdam. She also remembered watching the endless stream of Jews who were marched down the

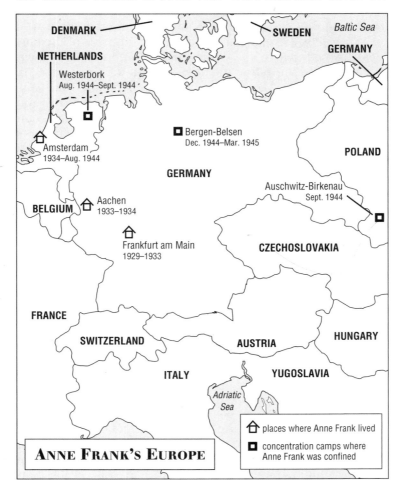

ANNE FRANK'S EUROPE

streets to be sent to work camps. Often the war brought shortages in food and supplies, and Anne would have to eat the same food every day. There were even occasions when the office building below was burgled, and the members of the annex feared they would be discovered.

Finally, that dreaded fear became a reality. The Green Police, a group of Dutch police organized by the Nazi occupation force, received an anonymous tip revealing the location of the Frank's secret hiding place. On August 4, 1944, the police came and arrested Anne and the other seven residents of the annex. They were all taken to the local jail and then moved to Westerbork transit camp in the Netherlands. One month later, all of the residents were transferred to Auschwitz concentration camp in Poland. Anne's mother and Hermann van Pels died in Auschwitz. Auguste and Peter van Pels and Fritz Pfeffer were each transferred to different camps, where they all perished. Anne and her sister were transferred from Auschwitz on October 6, 1944, to Bergen-Belsen concentration camp. There they both became very sick with typhus, a disease common in overcrowded, unsanitary confines. First Margot succumbed, and then a few days later, in February or March of 1945, Anne died. Of the eight members of the Secret Annex, only Anne's father survived Auschwitz.

SIMPLY A YOUNG GIRL BUT HARDLY TYPICAL

Anne is revered today. She stands for the many innocent victims of the Holocaust, particularly the children. Yet, she was hardly typical of the millions of Jews who endured the Holocaust. Unlike many of the Jews in Holland during the war, her family was wealthy enough to be able to make plans. They might have been able to get away from Amsterdam altogether had they recognized the threat early enough. They were fortunate that at least four friends were willing to risk their own lives to hide them for over two years. Not many Jews were able to rely upon the charity of others. Furthermore, most Jews were separated from their families as they sought to evade Nazi persecution; the Franks were able to stay together until their arrest. All of these factors contributed to the uniqueness of the experience that Anne had before her arrest and death.

The strength of Anne's family, particularly her father, gave her courage throughout the grim reality of war. While many other Jews lost what little they had, Anne was able to survive and continue learning and growing during this time. Anne was not the only child who lived in these extraordinary times, nor was she the only one who kept a diary. But thanks to Miep Gies, Anne's diary was saved from destruction. After the family's arrest, Gies went back into the annex. The Gestapo had taken everything of value but had simply thrown Anne's diary to the ground. Gies gathered the papers and locked them in a desk drawer, in the hopes that she could return them to Anne. Of course, Anne never returned.

ANNE'S LEGACY

When Otto Frank was liberated from Auschwitz and returned to Amsterdam, he knew that his wife had died, but remained hopeful that his daughters were still alive. When he learned that they, too, had perished, he felt that he had lost everything. Miep Gies, however, gave him Anne's diary. Otto latched on to this memento of Anne, and he translated sections of the diary into German for his friends and distant relatives who had survived the war. The diary generated so much interest that he decided to have it published, and suddenly young Anne Frank, who so desired to be remembered after her death, became known throughout the world.

Part of Anne's legacy is that her diary is an accessible introduction to the Holocaust. The intimacy of her writing leaves readers with a feeling that they truly do *know* Anne. She is more than a statistic or faceless victim. Her temper, her playfulness, her dreams, and her desires all strike a chord with readers who recognize how tragic it was for such a vivacious and talented spirit to be snuffed out by prejudice and hatred. Anne wrote eloquently of her emotions and thoughts, and it is this that helps readers identify with the young girl who simply wanted to be a writer.

Her great potential is another aspect of Anne's legacy. She was a talented writer and certainly might have furthered that talent had she survived the war. Though she was realistic about the war and the pain it caused, she did not allow that negativity to kill her optimism, thus inspiring others never to give up hope. This is her legacy.

NOTES

1. Mirjam Pressler, *Anne Frank: A Hidden Life,* trans. Anthea Bell. New York: Dutton Children's Books, 1999, p. 53.
2. Anne Frank, *Anne Frank: The Diary of a Young Girl,* trans. B.M.

Mooyaart-Doubleday. New York: Pocket Books, 1972, p. 11.

3. Frank, *Anne Frank: The Diary of a Young Girl*, p. 2.

4. Miep Gies and Alison Leslie Gold, *Anne Frank Remembered: The Story of the Woman Who Helped to Hide the Frank Family.* New York: Simon & Schuster, 1987, p. 123.

5. Frank, *Anne Frank: The Diary of a Young Girl*, p. 97.

6. Frank, *Anne Frank: The Diary of a Young Girl*, p. 58.

7. Frank, *Anne Frank: The Diary of a Young Girl*, p. 58.

8. Frank, *Anne Frank: The Diary of a Young Girl*, p. 177.

9. Gies and Gold, *Anne Frank Remembered*, p. 186.

CHAPTER 1

IN HIDING

A New Life in Amsterdam

Melissa Müller

When European journalist Melissa Müller reread
Anne Frank's diary as an adult, she was curious to
know more about the young girl. Her many questions
led her to a journalistic investigation, and eventually
she compiled *Anne Frank: The Biography*, the only
full-length biography of Frank's life. Müller had access to exclusive interviews and documents, which
provided her with a greater understanding of Anne's
short life. This excerpt from a chapter on four-year-
old Anne describes how her family moved from
Frankfurt, Germany, to Amsterdam, Holland, to escape the oppression of Jews in Germany. Müller not
only provides details about Anne's personality,
friendships, and experiences during these years prior
to going into hiding, but also how she and her family
adapted to their new life. There is little written about
this period of the Frank family's life, so this article is
especially important in revealing the background
against which Anne would begin her diary.

Anne Frank was not a retiring child. She demanded constant
attention—or so it seemed to her parents. She was inquisitive,
asking one question after another and refusing to be put off
with partial answers. If she asked "Why?" she expected a full
and detailed response; if she didn't get it, she was deeply hurt.
But when Anne the tormentor tilted her head to one side, low-
ered her eyes, faked a bashful smile, and batted her eyelashes,
no one could resist her, least of all her father. Curiosity, humor, and an adventurous spirit sparkled in her big greenish
eyes, made all the more expressive by their dark brows and
long lashes. She loved company, fun, constant activity. Otherwise, she grew fidgety. She was headstrong and mercurial.

Melissa Müller, *Anne Frank: The Biography*, translated by Rita and Robert Kimber.
New York: Henry Holt and Company, 1998. Copyright © 1998 by Melissa Müller. Reproduced by permission of the publisher.

Thwarted, she'd resort to tears in order to get her way.

On Tuesday, June 12, 1934, she was even more excited than usual. It was her birthday, her fifth, and the first she would celebrate in her new home. In the afternoon, she had her new friends over for a birthday party—a family tradition the Franks brought with them from Frankfurt. Among the guests was Hanneli, with whom Anne attended kindergarten; Sanne, who lived around the corner; and Juliane, who was two years younger and lived one flight up from the Franks. [Anne's older sister] Margot had also invited her classmate Barbara, Sanne's older sister. Each of the girls brought Anne a present and received a little favor in return. Juliane, for example, took home a tin tea service for her doll kitchen.

Anne was the perfect hostess. She swept the others along with her enthusiasm and her infectious giggling. Her lively prattle was still mostly in German, but Dutch words had begun to crop up in her speech.

ANNE'S ARRIVAL IN AMSTERDAM

She had come to Amsterdam from Aachen only four months earlier, as a surprise for Margot, who had been living in Holland for two months. Margot had celebrated her eighth birthday on February 16, and when she came into the living room she found her little sister all dressed up and sitting on the table piled high with gifts. In a white tutu, and with her hair cut short like that of a street urchin, Anne took part in Margot's little birthday party. She was remarkably quiet and reserved, awed by the new faces and new surroundings.

But her shyness did not last long. "Anne has made the adjustment better than Margot," Edith Frank wrote in July to Gertrud Naumann, with whom she continued to maintain an active correspondence. Anne's first weeks had not been easy. Edith Frank did her best to make the transition as smooth and painless as possible. She hoped their lives would settle down and that her children's routine would quickly resume. But whereas Margot went to school every morning and came home happy and full of stories, Anne was lonely for her friends in Frankfurt and Aachen and the company of other children. She begged her mother to let her go to kindergarten, but it was already full. To keep her busy, Edith sent her back to Aachen several times to visit her grandmother and uncles.

ANNE BEGINS SCHOOL AND MAKES FRIENDS

By May, however, there was room for Anne in the kindergarten and she began attending the Montessori school on Niersstraat, a ten-minute walk from home. On her first day there she made friends with a girl named Hanneli Goslar, who spoke German and, like her, had been living in Amsterdam only a short time. Anne had already seen her and her mother in a shop a few days earlier. Anne's mother and Ruth Goslar, delighted to find that they both spoke German, had struck up a conversation and discovered that they lived next door to each other on Merwedeplein. The children, in the meantime, had eyed each other with interest.

When Hanneli arrived at the *Kinderhaus,* as the preschool classes at the Montessori school were called, Anne was already there. Among the many unfamiliar children speaking an incomprehensible language, Hanneli was relieved to find not only one she knew but also one who spoke German. She headed straight for Anne, who gave her a welcoming hug. Absorbed in each other, the two girls completely ignored their worried mothers, who had braced themselves for whining and tears. "Anne really enjoys going to kindergarten now," Edith could report.

In no time Anne had made many friends. Her cheerfulness, inventiveness, and love of mischief made her popular. She showed her domineering and possessive side only when she didn't get her way. Anne's best friends, Hanneli and Sanne, probably didn't mind Anne's taking the lead. Hannah Elisabeth Goslar—Hanneli to the other German children but Lies to her Dutch schoolmates, who could not pronounce Hannah—was six months older than Anne. She was considerably taller but just as delicate—indeed, skinny—and wore her brown hair in ringlets. She was extremely gentle and shy. Susanne Ledermann, whom Anne called Sanne but whose parents and sister continued to call her the more German Susi, was also about six months older than Anne. A quiet, intelligent child, Sanne was less volatile and playful than Anne; even when she smiled her dark eyes seemed serious. The trio of girls, soon inseparable, was known as Anne, Hanne, and Sanne.

ANNE'S HOME IN HOLLAND

Merwedeplein was the center of the River Quarter. Unlike the leafy neighborhood around Ganghoferstrasse in Frankfurt, which was a paradise for children, this triangular plaza was urban and rather bare. . . .

Later, the plaza was landscaped. Symmetrically placed shrubs and trees separated the asphalt of the street from the lawn in the center. The grass was not, however, a delicate decorative variety but a rugged turf suitable for a playground. On Amsterdam's rare sunny days, the neighborhood children would be out on the Merwedeplein, those who lived on the left side in a separate group from those who lived on the right. It was not particularly easy for newcomers to join in, unless they happened to be as outgoing and self-confident as Anne.

A child who wanted to pick up a friend to play would not knock on the door or ring the bell but whistle a tune agreed upon beforehand. Anyone who could not whistle—and Anne, with her overbite, could not—had to resort to something else. If Anne wanted to call a friend to play, she had to sing the tune.

In the trees and shrubbery and on the grass in the middle of the plaza, the children played hide-and-seek, tag, and catch and shot marbles. There were always enough children for games like stickball. The girls did handstands and cartwheels and jumped rope. On the sidewalks they played hopscotch, raced about on scooters and roller skates, and rolled hoops, whipping them along with small sticks. . . .

THE FAMILIES BECOME FRIENDS

Edith and Otto Frank cultivated friendships with families they knew from Frankfurt but actively developed new ones. They soon became close friends with the Goslars and the Ledermanns. . . .

That the three families had moved in separate circles at home hardly mattered in this new country. The Franks were invited to the Goslars every Friday evening, sometimes for tea or coffee after dinner and often for dinner. The Sabbath candles would already have been lit, and Hans Goslar would have just returned from services at the synagogue and blessed his daughter, Hanneli. It meant a great deal to Edith Frank to participate in the Sabbath ritual at the Goslars. Hans Goslar pronounced the Hebrew blessing over the kiddush cup before the Sabbath meal, washed his hands in the special bowl, and, finally, blessed the two braided Sabbath loaves and passed pieces to everyone at the table. These were the same Friday-evening rituals Edith's parents had observed in her Aachen home. She had not missed them in Frankfurt, but now, in exile, they gave her strength and a sense of continuity in this alien, bewildering environment. Otto, however, was unfamiliar with religious Judaism and did not understand the Hebrew blessings. He had not even been bar mitzvahed. Nonetheless, he listened attentively and respectfully on these Friday evenings.

Edith would have liked to invite the Goslars to her home, but Ruth Goslar, at her husband's request, kept a kosher household, and the Goslars could not have eaten anything at the Franks'. In fact, Ruth Goslar rarely attended the afternoon coffee circles that the immigrant wives held at the Franks' and in other apartments, though not, primarily, for religious reasons but because she worked all day as her husband's secretary and had no time for such small pleasures. . . .

ANNE ENROLLED IN A LIVELY SCHOOL

"Imagine. Today I have to register Anne at school," Edith Frank wrote to Gertrud Naumann on March 26, 1935. "Anne will probably continue on in the Montessori school." The pedagogical principles that Maria Montessori had developed thirty or so years earlier, with their emphasis on self-motivation and individuality, were perfectly suited to a strong-willed and obstinate child like Anne Frank. Eschewing the conventional division of children into grades, the system allowed more tolerance both for those who were ahead of their age group and for those who were behind. At the start of each school day pupils chose what they would do, whether alone or in a group. Anyone who wanted to draw could draw, anyone who wanted to do arithmetic could play with an abacus; the main thing was that the pupils concentrate on whatever they had chosen to do. Anne read a lot. She had begun reading a few months earlier, probably imitating Margot. In January 1935 Edith Frank had written to her family, "Anne is learning to read with great difficulty." "With great difficulty" was underlined. . . .

Anne, playful, lively, and easily distracted, enjoyed school and the freedom her teacher, Jan van Gelder, a moderate Communist, gave the children. They were allowed to do almost anything and were required, so it seemed, to do very little. In Anne's class, almost half the children were Jewish, many of them from German families. The school made considerable allowances for these children, who were slowly ridding themselves of their accents. The teachers did not make excessive demands of them but gave them time to adapt to their new surroundings. Anne—Annelies to her Dutch schoolmates—was not forced to struggle with arithmetic much, for example. Nor was Hanneli, who was called Lies, or their friend Kitty. There were plenty of other things to do. Anne began writing stories very early. Kitty displayed a remarkable talent for drawing and liked to arrange words and letters in patterns that suited her playful visual imagination, sometimes running all the words in a sentence together, other times spacing the letters far apart. The Montessori school not only tolerated such unorthodoxy but encouraged it. When arithmetic was the order of the day, it was taught in the form of a game. If, for example, Mr. van Gelder asked the children what two times one was and no one knew the answer, he would take the children by the hand one at a time and hop with them up and down the rows of desks, counting as they went. Two hops times one was two. Three hops times two was . . . six. There would be smiles all around.

A WARM, HOSPITABLE HOME

Children from Orthodox families were not required to attend school on Saturdays. Sol Kimmel was among them, a small, chubby boy with blond hair and blue eyes. Even as a five-year-old, Anne was drawn to him, perhaps because he had no father and she felt sorry for him or because he could be very funny; at any rate, she decided she would marry him. His cousin, Ab Reiner, was slim and dark-haired and clearly the more attractive. He, too, was absent from school on Saturdays, as was Hanneli Goslar, with whom Anne, once she was considered advanced enough for nightly homework, made an agreement that she kept for the rest of their time in school. They never saw each other on Saturdays, which Hanne spent with her Sabbath friend Ilse Wagner and Anne spent with Sanne, who went to a different school. But every Sunday, after Hanne had come home from her religion lesson, Anne gave her the previous day's assignment. Then they played together, either at the Goslars' or at the Franks' apartment.

The Franks kept a warm, hospitable home where their daughters' Dutch and immigrant friends were always welcome. Children loved to visit the Franks' house: life seemed more elegant than it was at home. Mrs. Frank served delicious rolls topped with cream cheese and chocolate bits, cold lemonade, and bottled milk, a particular treat. Ordinarily, grocers ladled milk from a large can into jars that customers brought with them to the store; bottled milk was more expensive. The Franks even had central heating—a rare luxury. And if you stayed for a meal, the dining table was equipped with a lazy Susan you could spin around and choose your dishes from. Water was served with the meal. That in itself delighted Hanneli, who at home was allowed to drink water only after meals. At Anne's, too, she could be freer about the Jewish dietary laws, which her parents did not expect her to observe as strictly as they did.

The greatest delight of all was Mr. Frank. His wife was always there and always friendly, but the children hardly noticed her; they took such things for granted in mothers. But Otto Frank, at almost six feet a tall man for those days, was special. With Mr. Frank you could talk and joke about anything. He made up games, told stories, always had a comforting word, and seemed to forgive Anne everything, even when she was stubborn and insisted on having the last word. Margot and Anne adored their father, whose close-cropped moustache and fringe of thinning hair were already turning gray. Their adoration was well-founded. Otto's high spirits were truly infectious. And when he was at home he spent more time with his children than most other fathers did. . . .

[Edith] was also a busy hostess. Unobtrusive, almost unnoticed, remaining in the background, she was nonetheless responsible for the pleasant domestic atmosphere. And she was constantly concerned about Margot and Anne's health.

CONCERN FOR ANNE'S HEALTH

Anne especially was prone to illness and often bedridden. "Anne still has to spend time in bed because of a lingering flu she came down with in October," Edith wrote on December 27, 1935. "But fortunately she has recovered well in recent days. She gets up often during the day, enjoys being spoiled, and doesn't miss school much. Her teacher, an extremely nice man, came to visit her not long ago." But the delicate girl—who, despite her rambunctious temperament, had acquired both at home and at school the nickname *Zärtlein* (fragile one)—was often absent for weeks at a time. At first she had the usual childhood illnesses—whooping cough, chicken pox, and in December 1936, measles. Then came a constantly recurring fever that, though mild, nonetheless sapped her strength. Anne had heart trouble, some people said. Maybe she had been a blue baby, others theorized. Still others suspected rheumatic fever.

At the beginning of 1937 Anne was sick again, but on January 18 Edith could write, "Anne was out on the street for ten minutes today for the first time, and we hope she'll continue to recover well." But not until a year later, in the spring of 1938, could her mother breathe a sigh of relief. "We're delighted that Anne is somewhat stronger now." Still, the frail-looking child had to be careful. In gym she almost always sat on the spectators' bench, though not entirely because of her fragile constitution. She had a trick shoulder and couldn't do somersaults or cartwheels for fear of dislocating it. But throwing her shoulder out was evidently painless, because once she had mastered the art of popping it in and out, she entertained her friends with her new talent. She liked astonishing her schoolmates—and making them wince. Most of all, she liked being the center of attention.

On the Eve of Anne's Disappearance

Isabel Reynolds

Isabel Reynolds is a staff writer for a Japanese daily English-language newspaper, *Daily Yomiuri*. In this article, Reynolds interviews one of Anne Frank's childhood playmates during the opening of an exhibit in Tokyo which documented Anne's life. As the interview reveals, even as the Nazis were imposing increasingly restrictive rules on Jews in the Netherlands, Anne Frank remained a carefree young girl who enjoyed having friends. Jacqueline Sanders-van Maarsen (Jopie is her nickname in Anne's diary)—the interviewee—was one of Anne's best friends. Van Maarsen relates the story of how she and Anne met and became the closest of friends during the ten months before Anne went into hiding. After she learned of Anne's death, van Maarsen vowed never to use her friend's name to become well known herself. By sharing the stories she does of Anne's personality, the things they talked about, and the games they played, van Maarsen provides a unique snapshot of Anne just before she went into hiding.

For 10 short months in Nazi-occupied Amsterdam, two innocent young girls enjoyed a close friendship. Just like any other 12-year-old schoolfriends, they chatted about boys and books and played games together. The quieter of the two girls was named Jacqueline Sanders-van Maarsen; her vivacious pal was Anne Frank.

Van Maarsen is currently in Tokyo to mark the opening of an exhibition at Matsuya department store in Ginza devoted to her famous friend. In an interview at the store, she described how she met Anne on their first day at the special school that Jewish children were forced to attend.

"I can tell you how we met first, because it was very typical of Anne. After the first school day she came bicycling behind me . . . called me by my name and she said, 'You are in my class, are you also going this way?' and it turned out we lived very near to each other. . . . She asked me to come home with her and introduced me to her mother and her sister as her new schoolfriend immediately," van Maarsen said, smiling.

The two girls hit it off straight away, and Anne wasted no time in establishing rights over her new confidante. "The next day she decided, she said, 'Now we are best friends,' and I agreed. That was how Anne was. I am quite different. But I liked her, the way she behaved, and so we were so different, but at the same time we had the same interests and read the same books," van Maarsen said.

"We talked a lot, Anne especially, about boys, which she was very interested in. And sex was also a subject that interested her a lot. Which I never told anybody—30 years ago I didn't talk about this, but now I don't care any more. Anne writes herself about feeling each other's breasts, which I didn't want to do. So in that sense she was grown up, perhaps. We played Monopoly, on the board that is still here in the exhibition," she recalled.

ANNE'S GREAT HONESTY

At that point, van Maarsen had no idea that Anne possessed a latent talent for writing. But the relationship was from the beginning one of great honesty, a quality also evident from the diaries.

Both girls were too young to understand the enormity of what was going on around them, but they did feel a sense of unease at the growing restrictions placed on the Jews. As time went by, Jewish people were prevented from owning their own businesses, riding on trams or in cars, and were made to wear yellow stars to identify themselves. So the two friends agreed that if either of them were forced to flee the country, they would be sure to leave a farewell letter for the other. In fact, it was not until after the war had ended that van Maarsen finally received the note Anne had written to her.

Anne's family went into hiding in summer 1942, bringing the friendship to an abrupt end—even Anne herself did not know about the plan until the last minute, and her parents forbade her to mention it to anyone.

HER FRIEND DISAPPEARS

When van Maarsen realized that her friend had disappeared, she went to visit the deserted Frank house, to look for a farewell letter, and see if she could find Anne's diary. "I knew that she had written about me and I wanted to know what she had written, but it wasn't there, she had taken it with her," van Maarsen said. What was found in the house was a piece of paper with an address in Switzerland. Anne's father, Otto, had placed it there so that friends and relations would think they had managed to emigrate. Van Maarsen felt lonely without her friend but was at least convinced that she was safe.

In fact, of course, the Frank family was holed up in a few cramped rooms at the back of Otto's former company office, together with some other family friends. Their daily requirements for living were provided by loyal Dutch friends. Tragically, the hiding place was discovered after a couple of years, and Anne died of typhus at the Bergen-Belsen camp at the age of 15, along with her mother and sister.

Van Maarsen was luckier. Since she and her sister were Jewish only through their father, their mother was determined to get the girls reclassified as non-Jewish.

Her mother had heard rumors about the gas chambers and believed them, although most people refused to give them much credence. So, shortly after Anne's disappearance, she "went to the German authorities and she told them, 'I'm not Jewish.' She even lied to the Germans and said, 'My husband made me and my children Jewish without me knowing it,' which was not true, but she had to say something," van Maarsen explained.

Incredibly, this desperate plan was successful and the two young girls were able to remove their yellow stars.

NOT JEWISH ANY MORE

"So I was not Jewish any more. The first half of the war I was Jewish, the second half I was not Jewish any more and I came into a quite different atmosphere," van Maarsen explained. Even her father was allowed to take off his yellow star, although his identity papers were still stamped with a letter J for Jew. This was a very unusual privilege, and van Maarsen feels sure it would have been withdrawn, had the war lasted any longer.

She transferred to a school for non-Jews, just as the last of her old schoolfriends fled the country, went into hiding, or were imprisoned by the Germans. It took her some time to make new friends, but she was comforted by the thought that Anne was safe.

THE TRUTH COMES OUT

It came as a terrible shock when, some time after the end of the war, Otto Frank visited the van Maarsens and broke the news that the rest of the family was dead.

"I was 16 years old. I wanted to forget the whole war and all the awful things. We were liberated and I thought, 'Now I am free and I want to be happy.' But I couldn't be happy, because first of all I heard from Otto that everybody was dead and what had happened. Then my whole family, my father's family had been taken away and they didn't come back," she recalled.

Later, Otto visited again, bringing excerpts of Anne's diary, but van Maarsen hardly had the heart to read them. It was not until the edited diary actually appeared in book form that she read the whole story.

"I was too close to Anne to read it objectively," she admitted. "I didn't understand what impact it would have. I thought it was little girls' stories."

When the diaries became a worldwide best-seller, van Maarsen was reluctant to take advantage of her knowledge of Anne. Unlike the young diarist, she had always been unwilling to become the center of attention. She even told her children not to mention the friendship to anyone at school. Finally, 10 years ago, she decided to write her own book about her wartime experiences, after she became frustrated by the fact that other people were making up stories to sensationalize Anne's life. Nowadays, she has lost any trace of self-consciousness—she mentions that Anne would have been very surprised to see how she turned out.

"Anne is a good example," she said. "An innocent child who was a victim because she was Jewish. And then one can tell the whole story and it is easier for them to understand when it is just one child, whom they begin to love because they read the diary."

The Secret Annex

Ernst Schnabel

In the 1950s, author Ernst Schnabel interviewed
many of those who knew the Frank family. He collected these interviews into one of the first comprehensive books about Anne Frank, *Anne Frank: A Portrait in Courage.* Using his own research and the
memories of those he interviewed, Schnabel details
Anne's childhood, her time in hiding, her arrest, and
beyond. In this excerpt, Schnabel writes about his
experiences during a stay in Amsterdam. He visits
the building on Prinsengracht where Anne's family
was hidden, and interviews several of the people
who worked there and who helped hide the family.
Schnabel intertwines his experience and his interviews with Anne's own descriptions and memories
excerpted from the diary (designated in this piece
by italics) in a unique verbal picture of the annex
where Anne hid for two long years.

The Old City [of Amsterdam] is stitched together by hun-
dreds of bridges large and small. Along the paved banks of
the canals stand linden and elm trees, and back of these the
narrow, tall-windowed houses of dark Dutch bricks, topped
by steeples and saw-toothed gables, and the shifting, incon-
stant light from the sea. And over all stretches the moodiest
of skies, lighter and faster-moving, but also heavier and
more portentous than the sky anywhere else in the world.

During my stay in the city, the weather changed. The hotel porter said: "Now we are going to have real Amsterdam
weather."

So we did. It poured for a full week. On the last day I
climbed up to the Westertoren [clock tower]. From the tower
the sky was like one vast swell of the sea. Rain poured out of
flying cloud fronts; then came light; then more clouds and
shafts of rain, and more light in the distance. The light and

Ernst Schnabel, *Anne Frank: A Portrait in Courage*, translated by Richard and Clara
Winston. New York: Harcourt, Brace, 1958. Copyright © 1958 by Harcourt, Inc. Reproduced by permission.

the shafts of rain looped and swooped over the city, and among them a few gulls flashed like white sparks. The streets and roofs were steeped in wetness, as if Amsterdam were on the point of sinking into the sea again.

SEARCHING FOR WHERE ANNE WALKED

I stood on the south side of the observation gallery that runs around the tower. The wall behind my back protected me slightly from the rain and hail. I was looking for a particular street down there in the city below, but I could not find it among the many that led from the clean, bright suburbs to the dark, intrigue-filled heart of Amsterdam. It must be one of them, I knew, one coming from the southeast. But had they walked along the canal? Or down Vijzelstraat?

Streets are mute.

So we walked in the pouring rain . . . each with a school satchel and shopping bag filled to the brim with all kinds of things thrown together anyhow. We got sympathetic looks from people on their way to work. You could see by their faces how sorry they were they couldn't offer us a lift; the gaudy yellow star spoke for itself. Only when we were on the road did Mummy and Daddy begin to tell me bits and pieces about the plan. . . .

. . . when we arrived at the Prinsengracht, Miep took us quickly upstairs and into the "Secret Annexe." She closed the door behind us and we were alone.

So Anne wrote in her diary. But pity and shame could have been felt on any street in this city, and I did not find the particular one, hard as I searched for it.

A VIEW OF THE HIDING PLACE

I walked halfway around the tower, to the northeast corner, and looked down Prinsengracht. I could see the house. It stands on the bank of the canal, about a hundred or a hundred and fifty yards from the tower. The Secret Annexe is roofed with black-painted tin or asphalt roofing paper, and in the yard, in front of Anne's and Peter's window, stands the huge chestnut tree, its wind-tossed top rising higher than the building itself.

From my favorite spot on the floor I look up at the blue sky and the bare chestnut tree, on whose branches little raindrops shine, appearing like silver, and at the seagulls. . . .

Now the chestnut tree was in full leaf. It looked black,

soaked with rain, dripping. The gulls, too, had vanished, retiring all at once before a new cloud front which was now approaching. It came; overhead there was a roar, and hail spat grayly down out of the streaming cloud. A veil of gray was suddenly drawn over the canal. For a moment the house and the black tree could still be seen dimly, as through hammered glass. Then they, too, were gone. The hail clattered against the copper dome of the tower. Something struck my head and lashed into my face, and I took shelter inside the tower.

THE COMPANY AND EMPLOYEES OF OTTO FRANK

The hiding place . . . [is] in the building where Daddy has his office. . . . Daddy didn't have many people working for him: Mr. Kraler, Koophuis, Miep, and Elli Vossen, a twenty-three-year-old typist who all knew of our arrival. Mr. Vossen, Elli's father, and two boys worked in the warehouse; they had not been told.

(*Diary*, July 9, 1942)

Mr. Vossen died in 1954. Mr. Kraler, who after Mr. van Daan's withdrawal took over the management of dealings between Travis, Inc. and the affiliated firm of Kohlen & Co., is now living in Canada. He has corresponded with me. But Miep, Elli, and Mr. Koophuis I spoke to personally. . . .

Mr. Koophuis has known Mr. Frank since 1923. They had met on business dealings in Amsterdam. Otto Frank would be coming from Berlin or Frankfurt; he was always going from one place to another. Koophuis describes him as lively and full of energy. He would appear in Amsterdam, and then by the next day he would be gone again.

"Then, in 1933, he suddenly appeared at the door again, and that was the beginning of our long, unreserved friendship," Mr. Koophuis says. "We were personal friends, too, but I suppose that does not particularly interest you."

In 1941 Koophuis took over Frank's place in the Travis company; otherwise the firm would have been confiscated or liquidated as a Jewish business. When the roundups began the following year, Frank often slept at the home of a Travis agent, or in the homes of other acquaintances. In those days he, like many other exiles from Germany, still received warnings from various officials in the Dutch police when danger threatened his quarter of town. A total stranger would suddenly telephone the Franks, say something, and hang up immediately. Naturally, only coded warnings were possible, since telephones could be tapped by the Gestapo.

The situation being what it was, Koophuis and Kraler advised Mr. Frank and Mr. van Daan, who was in similar peril, that the time had come to look about for a hiding place, in case the persecution grew worse. They proposed the rear building of their place of business on the Prinsengracht, since these rooms were used only occasionally as a laboratory and for storing office files. Laboratory work was no longer carried on, since nowadays they had no choice in raw materials; they poured into the spice mills on the ground floor whatever they were lucky enough to be assigned by the government economic boards.

The proposal seemed a good one to Frank and van Daan. But since Jews were forbidden to move or even to transport household goods through the street, they gradually had pieces of furniture, rugs, and other necessities removed from their homes, supposedly for cleaning and repairs. Actually, these articles were all taken to Koophuis's home and from there, when occasion offered on a Saturday evening after working hours, moved to the Prinsengracht and hidden in the Secret Annexe.

Miep says:

"Mr. Frank bowed to necessity. He resigned from the firm when the time came; he wore the star; he said nothing. He never showed his feelings. I can still see him as he came into the office one day, in his raincoat, and when he unbuttoned the raincoat I saw the star on his chest underneath it. I don't think he had one on the coat. We made an effort to talk with him and act toward him as we always had in the past, and as though it were perfectly natural for him to come to the office now, for we knew that he dreaded pity. It was his way to come to terms with his feelings silently. A very Prussian trait, really."

Elli, the youngest member of the firm, had not noticed the mysterious changes and preparations in the building. She may have seen furniture being brought in and carried up, but she did not put two and two together, and she asked no questions.

A Rush to Hide

During the first week of July, however, all the employees had a meeting in what had formerly been Mr. Frank's private office. Mr. Frank sat at his desk as he had in the past, and Mr. Koophuis told them the whole story. All promised to keep the secret. But none of them suspected that the move would take place that same week.

Mr. Koophuis says:

"They telephoned me Sunday afternoon, and that evening I went out to their home on Merwedeplein. A post card had come ordering Margot to report on Monday to the reception center for the Westerbork camp. So we said to ourselves: now there is no point in waiting any longer."

Mr. Frank says:

"We knew that they sent out these cards, and many people had obeyed the order. It was said that life in the camps, even in the camps in Poland, was not so bad; that the work was hard, but there was food enough, and the persecutions stopped, which was the main thing. I told a great many people what I suspected. I also told them what I had heard on the British radio, but a good many still thought these were atrocity stories. I remember that one day a girl came to say good-by to us, the daughter of friends, and she told us that she had packed her sketchbook into her rucksack. She was very good at drawing, and she said she wanted to have a few mementos, for later. . . ."

A BUSINESS AND A SAFE HAVEN

Number 263 Prinsengracht is a tall, narrow old Dutch brick building. Its windows are now blank and empty, for it is no longer occupied. Someone has chalked a few illegible words on the door. Bicycles lean against the wall. One of the lower panels in the door to the warehouse has been repaired at some time. The old panel was smashed in by burglars on April 9, 1944.

The front of the building has that quiet beauty which can be observed in so many of these old houses in Amsterdam. It comes from the perfect simplicity and the finely balanced proportions.

Aside from the door to the warehouse, the building has two narrow entrances. One of these, which was usually kept closed even when Frank still worked in the firm, leads to a small staircase which goes straight up to the second story, as is frequently the case in Dutch buildings. It is a steep, dangerous staircase. Behind the other door is a side entrance to the warehouse, and an ordinary staircase.

There is another door at the top of the stairs, with a frosted glass window in it, which has "Office" written in black letters across it.

The word can still be read.

That is the large main office, very big, very light, and very full. Elli, Miep, and Mr. Koophuis work there in the daytime.

The room is empty now, and seems almost a small public hall. The big windows of the façade are almost opaque with dust. The water of the canal and the trees are seen as through a gauze veil.

A small dark room . . . leads to a small somewhat dark second office. Mr. Kraler and Mr. Van Daan used to sit here, now it is only Mr. Kraler. . . .

From Kraler's office a long passage goes . . . up four steps and leads to the showroom of the whole building: the private office. . . .

The paint is flaking from the ceiling; strips of wallpaper depend from the walls. The window is heavily shadowed by the chestnut tree in the courtyard.

THE HIDING PLACE ABOVE

A wooden staircase leads from the downstairs passage to . . . a small landing at the top. . . . The right-hand door leads to our "Secret Annexe." No one would ever guess. . . .

The cupboard that was built against the door to disguise it has been pulled down. Nothing is left but the twisted hinges hanging beside the door.

I went through the door and turned left, into the Franks' room. It is a low-ceilinged room, empty, like the entire house. It smells of mice and of ten years' silence and neglect. Next to it, on the right, is the tiny, single-windowed room in which Anne and Mijnheer van Düssel lived. Along the wall on the right, where Anne slept, a withered bouquet of flowers lies on the floor. The superintendent told me that schoolchildren from Hamburg had paid the place a visit. A tattered, yellowed remnant of curtain still hangs at the window. Through the curtain the chestnut and the houses across the courtyard appear as in a dream—as it is shortly before awakening, when the dream begins to fade. But from outside this curtain was opaque and no doubt afforded good protection during the day. As I went out I saw, right beside the door of Anne's room, a pencil mark on the torn wallpaper. Next to it is written:

"A 42"

Mr. Frank used to measure his daughters, but the other

marks have been stripped off along with the wallpaper. Only this one is left. In 1942 Anne reached exactly to the tip of my nose. Later I measured the height on myself. Two years before the arrest she was about five feet two inches in height.

A DESCRIPTION OF THE ROOMS

The van Daans' room on the next floor is large and handsome. The view from the window here extends smoothly far out beyond the yard. . . .

    The stairs lead up to the attic, which has two small windows. By leaning out of one of them you can see the Westertoren, and the golden crown that tops it, with the silvery-gray dome showing red through slits, and the golden cross above that, and through the other window the crown of the big chestnut tree can be seen.

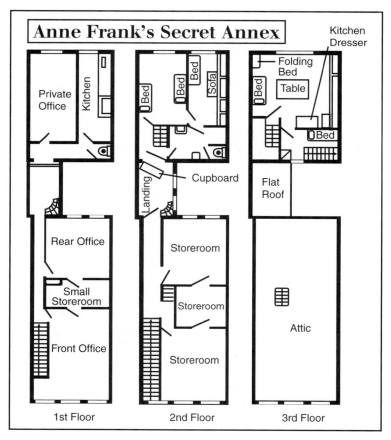

Anne Frank's Secret Annex

The loft window is always kept open at night now.
Evenings Peter and I often sit up there. . . . We are having a
superb spring after our long, lingering winter. . . . Our chest-
nut tree is already quite greenish and you can even see little
blooms here and there.

Now, in June, the blossoms of the chestnut have long
since faded. Standing at this window, I look out upon its
greenish-black foliage. One can see that this tree has been
loved. But the sky above it is blank. Or are there tracks in the
sands of the sky, only invisible?

THE IRONY OF THE ANNEXE

From the attic the windows of the houses across the courtyard can be seen. One of these must have contained the
apartment of the dentist whom Anne watched attending the
teeth of *an old lady, who was awfully scared.* And on the
right side of the yard, not thirty yards away, you look into the
back window of a house in which Descartes once lived—the
philosopher who declared: "I think, therefore I am." From
this very house he wrote to Jean Louis de Balzac, a friend in
France: "Is there any other country in which one can enjoy
freedom as enormously as one does here?"

The sentence is inscribed above the door of the house.

But the Prinsengracht house has no inscription on the
door aside from the number. Nevertheless, a girl from Japan
wrote to Otto Frank that her heart was in that house.

Countering Fear Through Faith

Rachel Feldhay Brenner

Rachel Feldhay Brenner is a widely published asso-
ciate professor of Hebrew and Semitic studies at the
University of Wisconsin–Madison. In this complex
essay, Brenner focuses on two Holocaust writers and
victims: Anne Frank and Etty Hillesum. Both lived in
Amsterdam; Etty Hillesum died in Auschwitz-
Birkenau, and Anne in Bergen-Belsen concentration
camp. (While the entire essay focuses equally on the
two women, this selection has been edited to high-
light Anne's life). Brenner argues that writing and
faith were a means of resistance against the persecution of the Holocaust.

Brenner considers Anne a "catastrophe Jew" because, though Anne was not an Orthodox Jew, she
identified herself with the Jewish race and particularly with the history of Jewish persecution and suffering. While Anne does not primarily write about
religion, or being Jewish, she does use her diary as a
place to face her fears and explore her relationship
with the divine. Ultimately, she sees God as something that can give her focus and strength to overcome the terror of living in hiding, as well as work
on her personal development. Brenner sees Anne's
writing and religious identification as important acts
of resisting the fear that the end might be near.

Both Frank and Hillesum were fully aware that their Jewish
identity made them targets of the Final Solution. . . . The two
women acknowledged their Jewishness and openly em-
pathized with the suffering that befell the Jewish people.

As was typical of "catastrophe Jews," both Frank and
Hillesum claimed their common fate with their people and

Rachel Feldhay Brenner, *Writing as Resistance: Four Women Confronting the Holocaust: Edith Stein, Simone Weil, Anne Frank, Etty Hillesum.* University Park: The Pennsylvania State University Press, 1997. Copyright © 1997 by Pennsylvania State University. Reproduced by permission.

pronounced their indignation about the humiliation and the suffering inflicted on Jews. In fact, we observe in their diaries that both Frank's and Hillesum's identification with Jewish suffering *as Jews* intensified with the aggravating situation of persecution.

Frank's and Hillesum's association with the persecuted Jews as their people needs to be reemphasized, especially in light of the critical views that question the genuineness of their Jewish response to the Final Solution. . . .

Such judgments of Frank and Hillesum are clearly inappropriate. These women were doomed to death for their Jewishness and struggled heroically to make some sense out of their fate and thus to maintain their humanity against terrible odds. Besides, the claim that they did not sense connection with the Jewish collective is far from being accurate. While it is true that, like most of the Western Jews, neither Hillesum nor Frank was a Zionist and that neither of them knew much about her Jewish heritage, it is difficult to dismiss either their genuine identification with the fate of the Jews or their sincere expressions of Jewish pride.

A Unique Identity

Frank communicates her sense of solidarity with Jews in no uncertain terms, affirming her faith in the chosenness of the Jewish people and acknowledging the uniqueness of her Jewish identity:

> We are Jews in chains, chained to one spot, without any rights, with a thousand duties. . . . If we bear all this suffering and if there are still Jews left, when it is all over, then Jews instead of being doomed, will be held up as example. Who knows, it might be even our religion from which the world and all the peoples learn good, and for that reason and that reason only do we have to suffer now. We can never become just Netherlanders or just English or any nation for that matter, we will always remain Jews, we must remain Jews, but we want it, too. . . . God has never deserted our people; right through the ages there have been Jews, through all the ages they have had to suffer.

. . . As "catastrophe Jews," both Frank and Hillesum place themselves in the context of Jewish suffering over centuries. They establish affinity with Judaism by identifying with the history of Jewish persecution. At the same time, they acknowledge the particular role of the Jewish people in the world. They accept the concept of Jewish "chosenness" as responsibility to serve as an ethical model for the world. It is significant that at the time when their own lives were in constant danger these assimilated Jews, who spoke neither Hebrew nor Yiddish, spoke unknowingly in the language of the old Jewish tradition of *tikkun olam*, mending the world, combining its universal message with their Enlightenment heritage.

UNDERSTANDING THE CATASTROPHE

The notion of moral responsibility even in a time of catastrophe indicates the desire to fend off the senselessness of the suffering. The "Jewish component" that emerges in their struggle against despair clearly communicates both a consciousness of Jewish identity and an acceptance of it.

As both diaries show, Frank's and Hillesum's sense of Jewishness was not confined to reading a historical-eschatological meaning into the unfolding Jewish destruction. Both Frank and Hillesum were completely aware of the unfolding Jewish genocide. In contrast to [historian] Geoffrey Hartman's claim that during the Holocaust "few could hope to make sense of the events, . . . [could] discern a normal pattern that could eventually be expressed in the form of a story," these women lucidly read the horrible narrative of the systematic destruction of the Jews in the events they witnessed. . . .

The diaries of Hillesum and Frank prove that the victims were capable both of understanding and of articulating in writing the implications of the atrocities they witnessed. . . .

Frank demonstrates her understanding of the global scope of the disaster in similar terms, when she writes: "No one is able to keep out of it, the whole world is waging war." She deplores the destruction of the city in the bombings, the wounded, the dead, and the lost children. She talks specifically of the catastrophic situation of the Jews, and tells of Jewish friends deported to Westerbork, and about the news of Jews murdered and gassed. She refers to stories "so gruesome and dreadful that one can't get them out of one's mind." She has nightmares of Jews "sent to filthy slaughterhouses like a herd of poor sick, neglected cattle."

Her sense of solidarity evokes tremendous guilt for being safe when other Jews are exposed to persecution. Forgetting her own incredibly precarious situation, Frank reports, "I saw two Jews through the curtain yesterday, I could hardly believe my eyes; it was a horrible feeling, just as if I had betrayed them and was now watching them in their misery."

These painful observations convey a full consciousness that the existence of Jews was coming to its end. They also clearly disconfirm the critical views that question Frank's and Hillesum's identification with the fate of the Jewish people. It is precisely the extent of their identification with Jewish suffering that raises the more pertinent issue of emotional adjustment to their horrific entrapment for being Jewish.

How did they cope with the unfolding narrative of total Jewish destruction? How did they fend for their sanity in a situation of mass murder "beyond comprehension," which one "can't get out of one's mind"? How did they contend with the awareness that their own death was inevitable? . . .

ATTEMPTS AT "PSYCHOLOGICAL SURVIVAL"

For [Frank and Hillesum], even a semblance of normal life was diminishing inexorably. To maintain normalcy in a world that had gone insane, they needed to construct an immune system, so to speak, that would protect them from growing fear and despair. . . .

Refusing to internalize the disgrace and shamefulness of the persecution emerges in Frank's *Diary.* On August 10, 1943, Frank writes down "a new idea." She will make believe that things are different from the way they are. She has decided to keep silent at mealtimes and pretend that the food she "simply can't stand" is delicious—and so, she writes, "before I know where I am it is gone." She applies the same technique to getting out of bed in the morning, which she had found "also a very unpleasant process." She gets up thinking "You'll be back [in bed] in a second," breathes some fresh air, turns the bed down quickly—and by then she would realize that "the temptation is removed."

In his insightful essay on Frank's psychological growth, John Berryman notes that in the entry just cited Frank aims at the two worst problems in her situation: the humiliating and exasperating situation of the meager and tasteless meals in the company of the irate others, and the hopelessness and fear to which she has to rise every morning. Berryman sees in Frank's responses to these morally debilitating problems an "ability to alter reality, to create a new reality, . . . one of her greatest mental strengths," which she puts "at the service of her psychological survival and tranquillity."

At its psychological level, Frank's and Hillesum's resistance to the increasing degradation takes the form of constant, disciplined modification of behavioral and perceptual patterns. To overcome the emotions of fear and distress, Frank and Hillesum employ intellectual sophistication and the freedom of imagination. . . .

Frank's celebrated statement that "in spite of everything . . . people are really good at heart" offers another example of a conscious attempt to modify the perception of a despair-provoking situation. In its context, the sentiment Frank conveys certainly does not confirm the naive message of hopeful faith in humanity that has been commonly attributed to this statement. In the sentence that follows, Frank admits that her belief in people "seem[s] so absurd and impossible to carry out." She confesses that she holds on to her ideals about the good in the world because she "simply can't" build her hopes on "a foundation consisting of confusion, misery, and death."

These disciplined attempts to modify emotional and intellectual responses represent extraordinary strategies of psychological survival. At the same time, it is important to emphasize that the two are women fully conscious of the situation against which they were erecting their defenses. Neither suppressed her understanding of the hopelessness of her position as a persecuted Jew. In a valiant attempt at

Female prisoners at Bergen-Belsen, the concentration camp where Anne Frank died.

what we might call "lucid self-deception," they tried to fend off the specter of despair. Their awareness of this self-contradictory psychological "game," which they nevertheless "played," communicates the extent of their determination not to give in to despair. At the same time, the paradoxical nature of this "game" of self-conscious self-deception signals both the vulnerability and the inadequacy of psychological means of survival.

FACING ALMOST INSURMOUNTABLE FEAR

To accept Frank's and Hillesum's attempts at character reformation at face value would attest to our reluctance to comprehend fully their desperation and fear, to our need to evade the enormity of their mental suffering. To perceive these attempts as the definitive evidence of the prevailing inner strength of the victims "despite everything" would trivialize the horror of the Holocaust experience. It is important to recognize that, even while trying to construct the "new reality," their efforts reveal the enormous odds against which they were trying to re-form their psychological selves.

Inner strength is "all that matters," claims Hillesum, reacting to the sense of "utter defenselessness"; I simply can't live with a sense of "confusion, misery, and death," asserts Frank. It is precisely the definitive tone of these statements that reveals the abyss of defenselessness, confusion, misery, and death that made it indispensable to construct a make-believe set of ideals to live/survive by.

Thus, the texts reveal the fragility of these mental defenses in the reality of deportations and concentration camps. The conscious efforts to erect barriers against fear communicate, in fact, the immensity of despair. In order to gain a measure of understanding of their hardship, we must try to fathom the fear that both women were striving to fend off. Only then will it be possible to gain insight into the images of God they construct in their distress.

CONFRONTING THE APOCALYPSE OF THE TIMELESS PRESENT

The similarity of the imagery that Anne Frank and Etty Hillesum use is striking. Says Hillesum: "From all sides our destruction creeps up on us and soon the ring will be closed and no one at all will be able to come to our aid. All the little loopholes that are still left will soon be stopped up." And Anne Frank has a nightmare in which "the clouds gather more closely about us and the circle which separates us from the approaching danger closes more and more tightly. Now we are so surrounded by danger and darkness that we bump against each other, as we search desperately for means of escape." The rhetorical patterns in these two quotations provide an inkling of the enormity of the fear and despair of the two women awaiting their fate. The emphasis on their complete, hermetic entrapment conveys the impossibility of redemption.

It is noteworthy that both Frank's and Hillesum's images evoke a global, all-encompassing catastrophe rather than a personal disaster. The emphasis on the totality and irrevocability of the approaching end in both descriptions evokes a sense of a universal, cataclysmic event that precludes any hope for survival. The images of the closing ring and the diminishing circle convey the sense of a sealed decree of complete destruction that will not spare a soul. Both writers represent their sense of approaching death in imagery that implies the apocalyptic ending of the world. . . .

As for all Jews in Europe, for Frank and Hillesum, history has assumed the apocalyptic dimension of timelessness, of death-in-life. Frank was very much aware that her life had become devoid of meaningful memories and purposeful planning. "I do talk about 'after the war,'" she says, "but then it is only a castle in the air, something that will never really happen. If I think back to our old house, my girl friends, the fun at school, it is just as if another person lived it all, not me." Time that lost its meaning—it alienated her from her past, and therefore from the sense of self. Because there was nothing to expect, life turned into a depressing routine underlain by constant dread of the end.

The dread of the end, as Frank experienced it at times, was overwhelming. In poetic, metaphorical language, she communicates the oppressive atmosphere, which is "as heavy as a lead," and "a deadly close silence [which] hangs everywhere, catching hold of me as if it would drag me down deep in an underworld." She sees herself as "a songbird whose wings have been clipped and who is hurling himself in utter darkness against the bars of his cage." At a later date, the desperation becomes even more pronounced, when she wonders, "How long have we still to put up with this almost unbearable, ever increasing pressure" and asks to "let the end come, even if it's hard." . . .

STRUGGLING TO RELATE TO GOD

The pervasive sense of the destruction all around them brought forth the question of the Divine, its potency, and its relationship to the world. Even as they tried to maintain their faith in ethics and humanitarianism, both Frank and Hillesum were struggling with the question of their relationship with God at the time of fear and despair.

In view of their humiliating and degrading exclusion from humanity, the two women needed to reaffirm their humanity in the consoling presence of the Divine. Despite the increasingly imminent end, and perhaps because of it, they searched with growing intensity to establish a sense of a God, which would offer meaning and consolation at the moment in which, paradoxically, the world—God's creation—was coming to its end. . . .

IMAGES OF GOD IN THE WORLD

Both Frank and Hillesum seek consolation and comfort in the Divine. Frank sees the consoling presence of God in nature: "Only then does one feel that all is as it should be and that God wishes to see people happy, amidst the simple beauty of nature. . . . Nature sets all fear at rest for every trouble, even when there are bombs or gunfire.". . .

These declarations of faith diverge from commonplace notions of the powerful, rescuing God. Frank does not pray to God to save her from the reality of "bombs or gunfire.". . .

The absence of the expectation that God might actually save from death, or at least alleviate the suffering, leads to a twofold realization. It communicates the two women's consciousness of the irrevocable apocalyptic reality they are witnessing and experiencing, and the uncompromising straightforwardness about the unfolding cataclysmic horror that will inevitably engulf them brings forth a concept of God who saves them *in* but not *from* the terror in which they live and die.

Because history had reached an apocalyptic point of no return, the God of Revelation could no longer fulfill his traditional providential role. In the reality of the Holocaust, the commanding God of history seemed to have absented himself from the history of the Holocaust. The God that both Frank and Hillesum invoke and pray to is not a God revealing himself as powerful, authoritarian God, but rather a God of loving attention and consolation. It is a God who does not

rescue the lives of the victims, but one who sustains the suf-
ferers in their struggle to maintain, as long as possible, a life
of dignity and self-respect.

NOT A TRADITIONAL JEWISH GOD

It seems important to reiterate that, as pictured by Frank and
Hillesum, the Divine is not a reflection of the Jewish God.
Against the critics who questioned their Jewish "authenticity," we discussed the pride that both Hillesum and Frank
have in their Jewishness, as well as their solidarity with
their victimized fellow Jews. However, the sense of belong-
ing to the community of persecuted Jews, and their faith in
Jewish chosenness to construct a better world, did not signify a conscious subscription to the Jewish concept of God.

At the same time, the God of Frank and Hillesum does not
conform entirely to the notion of the Christian God. It seems
that their discourse with God draws on ecumenical theol-
ogy, which stresses the universalist values of the Enlightenment era, values that emerge from both religious traditions.
Both Frank and Hillesum supersede the dogmatic distinc-
tions of religious concepts of God and conceive of a divine
entity, the essence of which lies in the ethics of dignity, self-
respect, and responsibility. Their God acts in self-revelation
by enabling them to transcend their fear and despair in a
perspective that reaches beyond the self.

Ostensibly, the ways in which they talk to God, even the
position in which they pray, reveal Christian undertones. In
one of the hard moments of fear and despair, Frank describes herself praying and crying "with my head on my
arms, my knees under me, on the bare floor, completely
folded up." Hillesum describes herself repeatedly as "the girl
who could not kneel." Finally she describes herself as "the
girl who learned to pray" with "folded hands and bended
knee." She admits it is a posture that "is not handed down
from generation to generation with us Jews."

Who is the God to whom they pray? What is the nature of
faith without the hope of survival? How meaningful is this
faith on the "different planet" of the Holocaust world ruled
by the forces of brutality and evil? "I know," says Frank,
"that I am not safe, I am afraid of prison cells and concentration camps, but I feel I've grown more courageous and
that I am in God's hands. . . . Without God I should long ago
have collapsed." Frank's fear projects an image of a God who

inspires faith despite the indubitable reality of the world changing into an enormous prison camp. We must recall that, when writing about Jews who will be held up as an example of the good after the horror is over, Frank did express a hope for the future. But when turning to her everyday reality, Frank discovers the faith that keeps her from "collapsing" in the here and now, amid the bombs, gunfire, and concentration camps rather than in an eschatological promise.

NATURE AS A REFLECTION OF GOD

For Frank, the concept of the Divine emerges in her understanding of nature as a reflection of God. Nature becomes the proof of God's existence, and its beauty and serenity attest to God's greatness. Frank finds a source of strength in nature, whose eternity supersedes the course of human history, which had reached a tragic, apocalyptic point of no return. God, who has disappeared at least temporarily from history, reemerges and is nevertheless present in the grandeur of creation.

In probably what is Frank's best and most moving short story, entitled "Fear," her autobiographical narrator finds God in communion with nature. In this story we recognize Frank's fear of being trapped in the Annex at the time of air raids in her fictional representation of the "grip of fear" that took hold of her at the time of shelling, shootings, and explosions. She describes how "fear clawed at my mind and body and shook me," how she escaped "from the fiercely burning mass about me," how she ran "with the image of the burning houses, the desperate people and their distorted faces before me."

In the end, the powerful sense of affinity with nature brings forth feelings of peace and comfort. The inner calm communicates God's loving presence: "When I was alone with nature, I realised . . . that fear is a sickness for which there is only one remedy. Anyone who is as afraid as I was then should look at nature and see that God is much closer than most people think.". . .

A GOD WHO CAN RESTORE HUMAN DIGNITY

Frank's God, whose presence she discerns in nature, is the God of loving care and of healing relief of suffering. In the story, the self-revelation of God in nature cures her "sickness." It reaffirms Frank's autobiographical protagonist's humanity at the time of dehumanizing terror. The message from God that she reads in the meadow, in the stars, in the dandelions, and in the clover leaves is healing because it reinstates her dignity and restores her self-respect, which was devastated by the haunting fear that has reduced her to a hunted animal.

In her perception of God, Frank demonstrates her uncommon maturity. Her meeting with God not in history but in the intimate aloneness in nature represents a concept of the Divine released from the strictures of religious denominations. Her concept of God is personal and not just historical. She structures the image of God through contemplation of the natural world, and at the same time redefines God's interaction with humanity.

On the one hand, nature reaffirms the existence of God despite God's temporary absence in history. On the other hand, as revealed in nature, the image of God that Frank discerns in nature differs from the traditional image of an omnipotent, commanding God. She meets God not in the human world but in the sphere of nature. Nature's beauty and tranquillity communicates a divinity that is benevolent, consoling, and healing.

The God that Frank discovers in nature is a God that each of us needs in order to be cured of the terrible "sickness of fear" that humanity has inflicted on itself. It is therefore no longer a communal God, but a personal God; no longer the omnipresent God who demands obedience, but a God whose presence depends on our readiness to find him. . . .

The compelling aspect of Frank's God is therefore the power to motivate the individual to seek morally restoring forces in her distress. As mentioned before, this God is not expected to prevent the conflagration of the world in apocalyptic destruction. Yet God has the power to empower the individual to seek self-dignity and self-respect in the world by recognizing herself as part of God's creation. It is not only the discovery of God in nature that heals the degraded self. It is, first and foremost, the compelling urge to commune with nature and to discern the divine immanence in nature that brings forth a renewed sense of self-worth. . . .

WRITING AND FAITH AS MEANS OF RESISTANCE

The notions of God, as they emerge in both Frank and Hillesum, are instrumental to their resistance of terror. God reveals himself in the motivation to construct a self potent enough to transcend the inner imprisonment of fear and despair, to break away from self-concern. This ability emerges in Frank's discovery of God in the beauty of nature and in Hillesum's realization of her inner self as the refuge of the defenseless God. God is close, yet he is Other; he is in me, or in my proximity, but it is up to me to find him. In order to give my attention to that which is not me, I must attain a measure of self-detachment that will liberate me from the confinement of the all-consuming terror.

Finding God, or finding the other, is therefore predicated on the ability to dissociate oneself from total absorption in the suffering, tormented self and to progress toward a more objective self-perception. The presence of God emerges in self-transcendence that liberates from fear and despair. How is this liberating self-transcendence attained? The art of autobiographical writing indicates an important avenue of liberation from the tyranny of dehumanizing dread and deprivation. In its employment of the faculties of the imaginative, the intellectual, and the ethical, the artistic quest for form, and the choice of life narrative and self-representation, signal defiance. Writing as self-discovery brings forth a liberating insight that transcends and thus relativizes the apocalyptic reality of the present.

Anne's "Otherness"

Denise de Costa

Dutch author Denise de Costa, whose field is women's studies, provides an analysis of Anne Frank and her diary from a distinctly feminist perspective. De Costa's book, *Anne Frank and Etty Hillesum: Inscribing Spirituality and Sexuality*, compares these two Holocaust diarists and victims. (The following text has been edited to remove sections specifically about Etty Hillesum, though some references to Etty remain.)

While much of what is written about the Holocaust is traditionally from the male perspective, de Costa focuses specifically on those ways in which Anne was not part of mainstream society. Being outside of what is socially acceptable makes someone what de Costa calls "the other." De Costa focuses on Anne as the other in two ways: as a woman, and as a Jew. In this excerpt from her introduction, de Costa points out that Anne was not traditional in her beliefs as a Jew, her thoughts about God, her role as a woman, or in her dream of a "career" as a writer. Through her diary and her short stories, she continually sought to mature herself personally and as a writer.

Anne Frank was a girl, Etty Hillesum a young woman. Both came from well-to-do Jewish families. Both lived in Amsterdam during the German occupation of the Netherlands, and both died in concentration camps—Anne Frank in Bergen-Belsen and Etty Hillesum in Auschwitz-Birkenau.

Both left behind diaries, letters, and short stories, which have drawn responses in the form of reviews, articles, novels, documentaries, music, plays, and visual art. By adding this book to the body of literature on their writing, I hope to change the process of canonization so that, from now on, their texts will be read differently. What I hope to contribute is a

Denise de Costa, *Anne Frank and Etty Hillesum: Inscribing Spirituality and Sexuality*, translated by Mischa F.C. Hoyinck and Robert E. Chesal. New Brunswick, NJ: Rutgers University Press, 1998. Copyright © 1998 by Marianne Denise de Costa. Reproduced by permission.

women's-studies perspective. "Women's studies" [is] an umbrella term for feminist research into the differences between women and men, or the feminine and the masculine. . . .

LETTING WOMEN'S VOICES SPEAK OUT

There has been little research into sex and gender differences at the time of the Holocaust. After all, the Nazis aim was to destroy all Jews, regardless of sex, age, social class, or any other factor which divided Jews themselves. Anne Frank saw her fellow Jews being deported from Amsterdam to the transit camp Westerbork:

> In the evenings, when it's dark, I often see rows of good, innocent people, accompanied by crying children, walking on and on, in the charge of a couple of these men, bullied and beaten until they almost drop. Nobody is spared—old people, children, babies, expectant mothers, the sick—they all join in the death march. . . .
>
> I get frightened when I think of close friends who have been delivered into the hands of the cruelest brutes the world has ever seen. And all because they are Jews.

To explore the differences of how women and men experienced and perceived the Holocaust would cloud the issue, because life and death did not depend on gender difference but on the difference between Jew and Gentile. It could also be argued, however, that by emphasizing differences, women's studies counteracts the rigidity of the Nazi conceptualization, which ultimately lumped all Jews together. Without losing sight of this context, women's-studies research into the Holocaust aims to let women's voices speak. . . .

WRITING AS A SAFE HAVEN

The writings of Anne Frank and Etty Hillesum have only been partly recovered. While the Nazis were doing their best to destroy the Jews, Frank and Hillesum were working on their personal development. Though their freedom to do so grew more restricted, language was a channel of expression no one could take away from them. Both devoted themselves to writing; in language they found a new home, a safe haven to which they could retreat.

While in hiding, Anne Frank began to seek an explanation for the war. At times she would draw the conclusion that God had foisted this hardship on the Jews. On those occasions, however, she also expressed faith that he would lift the suffering again. At other times, she placed the blame on people: "People simply have an urge to destroy, an urge to kill, to murder and rage, and until all mankind without exception, undergoes a great change, wars will be waged; everything that has been built up, cultivated, and grown will be cut down and disfigured, to begin all over again after that!"

Anne Frank was having bouts of depression, resulting from nearly two years of life indoors and various traumatic experiences. But she fought her despondent moods with a large dose of optimism. She clung to her dreams of the extraordinary future that awaited her: "I have made up my mind now to lead a different life from other girls and, later on, different from ordinary housewives."

In the Dutch, Anne actually wrote *lijden* (to suffer, to endure) rather than its homonym *leiden* (to lead), tinging this hopeful passage with bitterness. This excerpt dates from May 1944, just a few months before her arrest, which marked the beginning of her suffering in Westerbork, Auschwitz-Birkenau, and finally Bergen-Belsen.

"THE OTHER" AS A JEW

Anne Frank was confronted with the consequences of being "the other" in at least two ways. From a very young age, she had felt the effects of anti-Semitism. She was only a preschooler when her family decided to flee the Nazis. They left their hometown of Frankfurt am Main for Amsterdam. Seven years later, the Nazis occupied the Netherlands, and two years after that, the Franks went into hiding. Hence Anne knew very well what it meant to be Jewish, and in that sense to be "the other." She pondered this and discussed it with her boyfriend in the Secret Annex, Peter van Pels. Anne was dismayed when Peter turned away from religion: "Though I am not Orthodox either, it still hurts every time I realize how alone, scornful, and how wretched he really is."

She needed God in order to develop into a good person, while "upholding [her] own sense of honor and obeying her own conscience." Even though life was being made difficult for her because she was a Jew, she kept her faith.

"THE OTHER" AS A WOMAN

Anne Frank was "the other" not only as a Jew, but also as a woman. In the Secret Annex she became more aware of her sexually subject status and its inherent exclusions. In her diary she distanced herself from the traditional roles of house-wife and mother, but did so without denying her womanhood:

> I know that I'm a woman, a woman with inner strength and plenty of courage!

> If God lets me live, I shall achieve more than Mother ever has, I shall not remain insignificant, I shall work in the world for mankind!

She was not writing about the difference between men and women, but about differences between women: between girl and woman, mother and daughter. She did not want to be like her mother. She wanted, after the war, to see the world and to be financially independent. . . .

Anne had not yet begun to think about motherhood. She dreamed of a career as a journalist or writer. In the Secret Annex, she discovered a passion, linked to her Jewishness and her adolescence, for writing, from which she drew strength and comfort. One of the most important developments in feminism and women's studies in the 1980s is the recognition of how sexual difference is intertwined with other differences, such as ethnicity, class, and age. . . .

WRITING FOR PERSONAL DEVELOPMENT

In France, Hélène Cixous was one of the first to claim that her drive to write was fueled by a combination of her Jewish background and her womanhood. In *Coming to Writing*, she linked the desire to write with being in the position of "the other." She asserted that writing could be a reaction to discrimination or exile. Cixous herself had come from a society in which it was difficult for a Jewish woman to live in freedom, and there she discovered that writing could be an avenue for personal development. . . .

Anne Frank most certainly took the same route. Her diaries display a critical yet loving exploration of the self, in which she often saw herself as someone else in need of advice. But this someone else is the other in herself. . . . In her final diary entry, she described two sides of herself. One Anne showed herself to the outside world as a cheerful, bubbly, lighthearted girl, "nothing but a frolicsome little goat who's trying to break loose." The other Anne was more withdrawn and did not express herself in public but was much sweeter, purer, and wiser. This Anne did come out in the diary. For a long time she had hardly known this hidden side of herself. Before going into hiding, she had lived "a heavenly life," her days filled with admirers and girlfriends, with school adventures in the Amsterdam quarter known as the Rivierenbuurt. Then she was rudely cast out of this Eden. . . . She found it again both on earth (in her dream of becoming a writer) and in heaven (in her faith in God and her guardian angel). Writing in her diary was Anne's way of going into hiding internally, in order to remain or become whole. . . .

Anne Frank kept a diary for the entire period she was in hiding. In the spring of 1944, she began rewriting this diary after hearing a speech by Gerrit Bolkestein, minister of education, art, and science of the Dutch government-in-exile, broadcast by Radio Oranje. Bolkestein urged the people living under Nazi occupation in Holland to save their letters and diaries so they could be collected and kept for posterity. A few weeks later she decided to prepare her original diary for publication. She rewrote the entries on loose sheets in very neat and flowing handwriting. She made changes in style as well as content. Because she hoped that publication would earn her respect as a human being, but above all recognition as a writer, she tried to improve her writing style. For the same reason, she omitted certain passages that she considered unsuitable for publication, probably out of embarrassment. She left out nasty remarks about her mother and overt references to her own sexual awakening. In this way, she constructed herself as someone who conformed more closely to the dominant norms and values of the day. And thus, two Annes were born: the Anne of the original diary, who wrote only for herself, and the Anne of the second version, who was concerned with the preconceived notions of the outside world. . . .

It is especially interesting to see how Anne Frank censored her own diary. She left out the passages referring to her female identity, or more precisely, the process of becoming a woman: the conflicts with her mother, her increased awareness of her body and sexual feelings, and her first menstrual periods. Her father censored the diary along the same lines, sometimes at the explicit request of prudish publishers.

These facts are particularly interesting in light of the following paradox: Despite the fact that Holocaust-related literature centers more often on men's than women's experiences, the most widely read book about the persecution of the Jews is the diary of Anne Frank. However, this apparent contradiction is dissolved when one asks the question, "Which Anne Frank do we actually think we know?" The image propagated by the media has, to a great extent, been shaped to conform to conservative social values. . . .

Diary writing—an activity girls in particular are drawn to—appears to fill a void that is created by adolescence and, in Anne Frank's case, by forced isolation as well. Writing can serve to block out feelings of desperation and depression. . . .

I have tried . . . to reveal the importance of the mother-daughter relationship to the writing process. In discussions of how Anne Frank's parents influenced her development, Edith Frank-Holländer has always received less attention than Otto Frank. However, a psychoanalytic reading of Anne Frank's texts points toward a very different balance. In short, the realm of the feminine and the maternal is not abandoned upon entry into the symbolic order of language and culture; it continues to have an impact on Anne's development from girl into woman. Though this reading is a departure from the traditional reading reception-history of Anne Frank's diaries and her other writings, I demonstrate that her urge to write is best explained by the mother-daughter relationship, rather than the father-daughter relationship.

ANNE'S RELIGIOUS DEVELOPMENT

Although Anne Frank was persecuted for being a Jew, it is sometimes claimed that her Jewish background is a controversial issue because her family was not Orthodox and her writings display few Jewish elements. For example, Anne Frank and Primo Levi have been referred to as authors who owe their worldwide acclaim partly to "erasing Jews and Judaism in favor of humanity as a whole." In Anne Frank's case at least, I think the perceived lack of Jewishness has more to do with the reception of the diaries than with their actual content. . . .

Her religious development . . . left a clear mark on her diaries and stories. Anne Frank thought about believing or not believing in God, and about the relationship between Jews and Christians and between Orthodox and Reformed Jews, and she incorporated her ideas in her diaries and fiction. She also staked out a very specific position on the place of women in Jewish tradition. A psychoanalytical approach to her writings—with extra attention to apparently marginal,

light of this diary is the evidence of deep and growing insight toward the end into the meaning of the earlier disturbing emotions so honestly recorded. The meaning that Anne Frank found in her own development is remarkably similar to that given by Peter Blos and Helene Deutsch in their examinations of female adolescence.

The numerous interpreters of adolescence agree about the major tasks of that period: detachment from old love objects in the family; establishment of an independent identity, vocational as well as sexual; the ability to choose an appropriate heterosexual object with whom to establish a new family. The difficulties of such tasks are reflected in seesawing wishes for dependency and freedom; in the need for devaluation and hatred of the parents as weapons for attaining freedom; in the mourning and the object hunger that must accompany that struggle; in the narcissistic self-infatuation that helps to fill the emptiness and protect the sensitive ego, an ego suffering from the loss of the omnipotent parents and from awareness of its own limitations.

The special situation of the girl, as shown by Blos and Deutsch, revolves around the now dangerous tie to the mother, who represents a pull to the earlier dependent state. The resurgence of oedipal feelings for the father is in part a defense against such a tie, and since he must usually prove a disappointing ally, the girl may turn for comfort and for experiments with identifications to older women, to a girl friend, to a diary. Early, tentative reaching toward boys begins with idealizations, fantasies, and mutual projection of needs, but moves, hopefully, as sexual identity grows, to what Blos calls a ceding of sex-alien traits.

ANNE MATURES THROUGH HER DIARY

Keeping a diary may help, as well as portray, all of these processes; it might almost have been invented to meet adolescent needs. Blos mentions many functions the diary can serve: trying out new roles identifications; releasing tensions that might cause premature heterosexual acting out; aiding the ego to use its heightened awareness of inner life for recording, examining, and reflecting upon experiences and emotions. . . .

Although the impoverished environment may have been responsible for the great richness of Anne Frank's diary, the major themes are there from the beginning, before the need to go into hiding. Laments about isolation and loneliness, caused by pulling away from her family, punctuate the pages:

> . . . no one will believe that a girl of thirteen feels herself quite alone in the world.

> I can't refrain from telling you that lately I have begun to feel deserted. I am surrounded by too great a void.

> For in its innermost depths, youth is lonelier than old age. I read this saying in some book and I've always remembered it and found it to be true.

Anne addresses her diary as "Kitty" and knowingly uses it as a substitute for a girl friend. Even before fleeing her home, she has lost her friend Lies, who has become closer to another girl. Anne later looks back with anguish upon this event, . . . and never ceases to repeat, "If only I had a girl friend."

> . . . I want to bring out all kinds of things that lie buried deep in my heart . . . And now I come to the root of the matter, the reason for my starting a diary: it is that I have no such real friend.

ANNE'S RELATIONSHIP TO HER MOTHER

The strength of this longing is due in part to Anne's turning away from her mother and then seeing her mother as worthless in order to make the loss less painful and to lessen her feelings of inferiority:

> Mummy and her failings are something I find harder to bear than anything else. I can't always be drawing attention to her untidiness, her sarcasm, and her lack of sweetness . . . All this comes about because I have in my mind's eye an image of what a perfect mother and wife should be, and in her whom I must call "mother" I find no trace of that image.

Competitiveness and the need for feeling superior to the mother is clear:

> I face life with more courage than Mummy: my feeling for justice is immovable, and truer than hers . . . I shall attain more than Mummy ever has done, I shall not remain insignificant, I shall work in the world and for mankind!

Having needed to make herself a kind of motherless child, Anne then accuses her mother of being the one doing the abandoning; her guilt is reduced but her sense of deprivation is overwhelming:

> . . . I miss having a real mother who understands me. That is

why, with everything I do and write, I think of the "Mumsie" that I want to be for my children later on . . . To give me the feeling of calling Mummy something which sounds like Mumsie, I often call her "Mum"; then from that comes "Mums," the incomplete "Mumsie" as it were, whom I would so love to honor with the extra "ie."

Convinced that she is the injured, neglected one, Anne is freer to express her wish to be cared for. She justifies hurting her mother by refusing to say her prayers in her presence with the memory that her mother once rejected her company on a shopping trip. It is then the mother who is seen as preventing Anne from getting satisfaction of her needs:

Now it is suddenly clear to me what she lacks. Mummy herself has told us that she looked upon us more as her friends than her daughters. Now that is all very fine, but still a friend can't take a mother's place. I need my mother as an example which I can follow. . . .

But anger at the loss of the childhood gratifications alternates with anger at the threatening presence of such gratifications:

Mummy sometimes treats me just like a baby, which I can't bear.

I can't really love Mummy in a dependent, childlike way. . . .

ANNE TURNS TO HER FATHER

As safer substitutes for the dangerous objects, Anne passionately devotes herself to new interests: mythology, with its gods and goddesses; the Royal Family and its genealogy; and her own family tree, in which her father shares her studies. For a while Anne's attention focuses on her father, whom she sees as more worthy of her love than is her mother. He is a "darling": "I don't love anyone in the world but him."

He cannot, of course, sustain this role:

I cling to Daddy because it is only through him that I am able to retain the remnant of family feeling. Daddy doesn't understand that I need to give vent to my feelings over Mummy sometimes. He doesn't want to talk about it. . . .

At long last I have made the discovery that Daddy, although he is a darling, still cannot take the place of my entire little world of bygone days.

Only gradually and in retrospect are the bitterness and sense of betrayal, companions of the discovery, revealed.

Looking back upon her first year in hiding, Anne names as the greatest event the moment " . . . when I realized that even Daddy would never become my confidant over everything. I didn't want to trust anyone but myself any more."

And:

> How is it that Daddy was never any support to me in my struggle . . . Daddy tried the wrong methods, he always talked to me as a child . . . Why is it that Pim [Mr. Frank] annoys me?

ANNE FOCUSES ON HERSELF

It is while feeling deprived of both father and mother that Anne reverts to the process that Blos describes as the special narcissism of adolescence. In a state of object hunger, taking the self as a love object can mitigate emptiness and protect against a severe sense of inadequacy. Cathexes of the sense organs and a heightened ego feeling contribute to the inner awareness and increased creativity. Anne's diary permits the expression of such feelings and also stands as proof that she possesses a treasure of important thoughts and secrets.

> Who would ever think so much can go on in the soul of a young girl?

> I am young and I possess many buried qualities; I am young and strong and am living a great adventure.

> . . . we are much more sensitive and more advanced in our thoughts than anyone here would ever imagine in their wildest dreams. . . .

Observations and criticisms of the adults around her, the adolescent meddling that Deutsch describes, also provide material for the diary and a sense of self-importance:

> Why do grownups quarrel so easily, so much, and over the most idiotic things. Up until now I thought that only children squabbled and that that wore off as you grew up.

The dubious success of all these methods of defending against inferiority feelings is evident in the results of projecting these feelings; they naturally then seem to permeate the environment:

> . . . the horrible words, mocking looks, and accusations which are leveled at me repeatedly every day, find their mark, like shafts from a tightly strung bow, and which are just as hard to draw from my body.

> I'm not going to take all these insults lying down, I'll show them that Anne Frank wasn't born yesterday . . . Then they'll completely change their tune.

ANNE FALLS IN LOVE

Being in hiding fortunately did not deprive Anne of all non-family contacts, for the Franks shared their quarters with the Van Daans, whose son Peter was close to Anne in age. Anne describes as the greatest event of her second year in hiding a dream she had about Peter in which ". . . I discovered my longing, not for a girl friend, but for a boy friend." Still stung with rage and disappointment in her parents, Anne sees Peter with the eyes of someone not only lonely but needing to regain a sense of importance. This first heterosexual relationship is tinged with hostility and revenge, so that Anne excitedly records that her mother is jealous of her closeness to Peter, that her father disapproves, that Mrs. Van Daan too is envious. She now has a secret life more important than that of the diary. Deutsch has said that the young girl, feeling excluded from her mother's sexual life and wishing for equally interesting advantages, may see menarche as the magic key to adult status and secrets. Anne refers to menstruation as her "sweet secret"; she longs for it, as it "seems so important," and feels entitled to her relationship with Peter because she has been neglected by her selfish parents.

But soon after telling her father that his cruelty has made her turn to a new love, Anne perceptively sees that her attempt to show off and to "appear big" has distorted her feelings. Peter has been partly a reflection of such needs:

> My longing to talk to someone became so intense that somehow or other I took it into my head to choose Peter.

> I know very well that I conquered him instead of his conquering me. I created an image of him in my mind . . . I needed a living person to whom I could pour out my heart.

The attachment has been dominated by a looking-in-the-mirror quality; Anne finds in Peter what has been in herself: a desperation for someone to talk to, an angry boy who needs love. She sees as their greatest bond: "We both lack a mother." Their conversation is a perpetual, unflattering examination of their parents.

Yet Anne's success in attracting Peter, her ability to talk to him, help her grow away from her fear of worthlessness into a sense of sexual identity. . . . In the early days in hiding Anne and Peter unself-consciously entertain the adults by exchanging clothes, but much later Anne firmly states, "I know that I'm a woman, a woman with inward strength and plenty of courage."

BEING HONEST ABOUT HERSELF

Anne begins to have a sureness about being a separate person with both acceptable limitations and exciting potentialities, and her hostility to her parents starts to lessen in intensity. This permits the realization that earlier misery over them was powered by her own self-doubts. She movingly and honestly reflects:

> Now the trying part about me is that I criticize and scold myself far more than anyone else does. Then, if Mummy adds her bit of advice the pile of sermons becomes so insurmountable that in my despair I become rude and start contradicting, and then, of course, the old well-known Anne watchword comes back: "No one understands me."

The ego is still fragile:

> . . . I should completely lose my repose and self-confidence, which I have built up so shakily, if, at this stage, I were to accept criticisms of my half-completed task.

At fifteen Anne feels herself to be still incomplete, but optimistic about attaining identity as a writer and as a woman. The discovery and arrest of the Frank family, and Anne's subsequent death, are all the more tragic in denying her the fruits of her painfully-achieved growth, not quite won.

> I'm awfully scared that everyone who knows me as I always am will discover that I have another side, a finer and better side, I'm afraid they'll laugh at me . . . the "deeper" Anne is too frail for it . . . therefore the nice Anne is never present in company . . . I keep on trying to find a way of becoming what I would so like to be, and what I could be, if . . . there weren't any other people living in the world.

Anne's Experience in Hiding

Jacob Boas

In this selection, author and Holocaust historian Jacob Boas contrasts Anne's diary to those of four other teenagers who kept diaries during the Holocaust: Moshe Flinker, David Rubinowicz, Yitzhak Rudashevski, and Éva Heyman. Boas asserts that Anne's diary reveals that her life was, in many ways, easier than that of the children who were in the Jewish ghettos (communities that existed because Nazis forced the Jews to all live in one area). While the other young diarists were fighting for survival, Anne was able to continue a relatively normal life. She was a young girl largely hidden from the daily horrors that many other teenagers experienced during the Holocaust. Because of that, she was much more reflective, thinking and writing more about her personal development and growing up. Even in the midst of hiding, Anne continued to try to improve herself, to practice her writing, and to develop her beliefs about life, politics, and God. However, Boas does not discount that Anne's writing or experiences are important. On the contrary, he sees her constant introspection as encouragement to the diary's readers to "never give up hope."

The Holocaust knows countless hells but only one shrine. This shrine is located in the center of Amsterdam, and each year thousands of visitors clamber up the ancient building's steep and narrow stairs to have a peek at the cramped quarters where many years ago a young girl kept a diary while hiding from the Nazis. After twenty-five months, the hideout was betrayed and its occupants bundled off to annihilation camps. Only the father of the diarist survived. He and the diary.

Jacob Boas, "Anne Frank: I Must Uphold My Ideals," *We Are Witnesses: Five Diaries of Teenagers Who Died in the Holocaust*, edited by Jacob Boas. New York: Henry Holt and Company, 1995. Copyright © 1995 by Jacob Boas. Reproduced by permission.

Anne's diary is world famous. It has been translated into dozens of languages. It has been made into a movie and a play. It has inspired choreographers, composers, painters, and sculptors, even judges. Teachers use it in their classrooms. Presidents have quoted from it. She's the "world's most famous child."

Anne's fame is well deserved. She was articulate, perceptive, moving, humorous, serious. She was a fine writer. But hers is only one voice, while the victims were many; Anne's experience was unique, but so was that of her peers. The hunted included men, women, and children of all stripes, people with every kind of human response to suffering and terror. Her experience of going into hiding was unusual. Most Jews were holed up in ghettos, at the complete mercy of the killers. Alongside the other four diaries, Anne's looks different than when you read it by itself as the sole voice of the Holocaust. Sharing the stage makes her more human. Like David, Yitzhak, Moshe, and Éva, she was scared, vulnerable, and fighting with all of her heart to survive.

A Pampered Life

Anne, the second child of Otto and Edith Frank, was born on June 12, 1929, in Frankfurt, Germany, having been preceded by her sister, Margot, in 1926. . . .

Anne's father grew up in Frankfurt, a city with a reputation as an "island of tolerance." Otto Frank could not remember ever having encountered anti-Semitism in his youth. That would soon change. The Franks continued to live in Frankfurt until Anne was four. The year was 1933 and Hitler was in power. On April 1 the Nazis launched a campaign to boycott Jewish shops, and a week later there were laws banning Jews from the civil service and other areas of German life. Like many German Jews, Mr. Frank decided it was time to leave, crossing the border to explore business opportunities in Holland. The rest of the family soon joined him in Amsterdam, where he had started a firm supplying pectin to factories making jam. But seven years later Hitler followed in their path, and the good times were over. . . .

Anne's parents were decent, law-abiding, respectful of others, conventional. Like all parents, they wanted what was best for their children. Uncharacteristically, though, they considered their daughters' happiness to be more important than good grades. Margot and Anne grew up as moderns: independent, free-thinking, tolerant. "As for discipline—'The system is patience,'" Mr. Frank informed a "family-life expert" in a postwar interview. "Anne was sometimes difficult," and when she was little, they would occasionally give her "a quick spank," he confided.

Anne and her sister were pampered. In the last photograph taken of them before leaving for Holland, they wore furs, gloves, kneesocks, patent leather shoes, and hats. A picture in Margot's photo album has her sitting upright on a bed cuddling a stuffed animal and wearing dark aviator goggles to protect her eyes against the light of an ultraviolet sun lamp. When the family was taken by train to Westerbork, the camp in Holland from which they would be deported to Auschwitz, a fellow deportee "was amazed how well-dressed and well-cared for the Frank girls looked." The day they were dispatched to Auschwitz, they "looked as if they were going on a skiing holiday," recalled Janny Brilleslijper. "They had no idea what was in store for them."

LIFE IN HIDING

The fussing and fretting accompanied the girls into hiding. Every book Anne read had to be approved, though the rules were not very strict, she admitted. Nor was she allowed to have salt. As she got older, Anne grew tired of the kissie-kissie stuff and the cute little nicknames. "I think it's awfully annoying, the way they ask if you've got a headache, or whether you don't feel well, if you happened to give a sigh and put your hand to your head!" she quoted Margot as saying. In the course of writing about her "good and bad side," which happens to be the very last diary entry, Anne mentioned that every time she departed ever so slightly from the norm, when she was serious and quiet, for example, "my own family, who are sure to think I'm ill, make me swallow pills for headaches and nerves, feel my head and my neck to see whether I'm running a temperature, ask if I'm constipated and criticize me for being in a bad mood.". . .

For much of the time life in the annex was a series of greater and lesser vexations: rotting potatoes, lights that failed, beans that spilled, clothes that didn't fit, doctors' visits that had to wait, and so forth. But these were only "things." Far more troublesome were people problems. Because Anne was a terrific writer, it is easy to forget that her journal is a distillation of thousands of hours spent under prisonlike conditions. In addition to the run-ins with her parents, especially with her mother, for whom she expressed genuine aversion, Anne reported frequently on the penny-ante tortures she had to put up with every day: annoying adults; their incessant whining, bickering, and endless chatter about politics, food, and sleep; their strange capacity to find the same old jokes amusing or, alternatively, to sit glued to the radio listening to broadcasts endlessly repeating themselves, not to mention their irritating and disgusting habits, such as Dussel's snoring and her father's delight in adolescent bathroom humor. No wonder she yearned to be alone, for privacy and freedom of movement.

Anne Had a "Normal" Life

Yet compared with Éva, Yitzhak, and David, Anne led an almost "normal" life. She had books checked out from the library. She continued to receive fan magazines and to cut out pictures of her favorite movie stars. She experimented with different hairdos. In the early part of captivity, she felt rather like she was "on vacation in a very peculiar boardinghouse," and as late as May 3, 1944, she referred to her situation as "amusing," "a dangerous adventure, romantic and interesting at the same time."

The occupants of Prinsengracht 263 tried very hard to stick to their prewar routine. They had coffee at four, celebrated birthdays and various holidays, and continued to read Schiller and Goethe, eighteenth-century German writers whose works championed individual freedom and universal brotherhood.

Though it might have been reassuring, there was a flip side to clinging to set ways in the face of "the ever-approaching thunder." Most parents tried to find a refuge for their children away from cities, on farms, and in small towns, where they were less likely to be discovered, often deliberately separating them to maximize the chances that some might survive. By contrast, the Franks had opted to keep the family together in a warehouse where people worked in the daytime and burglars came by at night.

Anne's "Good Fortune"

When Anne turned fourteen, on June 12, 1943, her birthday was celebrated as though they were still living in freedom. There was a poem by Pim, and she "got very nice things," including a big book about Greek mythology, her favorite subject, and candy. The following year she received five volumes of art history, a botany book, underwear, two belts, a handkerchief, yogurt, jam, honeycakes, flowers, and so forth. Neither David Rubinowicz nor Moshe Flinker mentioned birthdays. Yitzhak Rudashevski remembered his only after it had already passed, using the occasion to take stock and to plan his future course.

All things considered, life in the "secret annex" was a good deal better than in the ghettos of Vilna, Bodzentyn, and Nagyvárad. Anne had enough to eat, even if the food was not always up to snuff. (Once, she had had so many strawberries she could not stand the sight of them.) Much of the time life in the hideout was simply boring.

Anne was not unaware of her good fortune. Like Moshe, whose situation most resembled hers, she felt guilty. "Cycling, dancing, whistling, looking out into the world, feeling young, to know that I am free—that's what I long for; still, I mustn't show it. . . ." Everybody in the annex was so self-centered, she complained, not excluding herself. Instead of saving "every penny to help other people, and save what is left from the wreckage after the war," they talked about the new shoes and clothes they were going to buy.

Anne had a probing, restless, inquisitive mind. Being shut in could not stop her from developing, and probably accelerated the process. As she argued in the letter to her father that she later regretted writing: "You can't and mustn't regard me as fourteen, for all these troubles have made me older. . . ."

ANNE'S MANY SIDES

Perhaps the most immediate benefit of life in hiding was the opportunity to give her penetrating mind free rein. Whether exploring the cause of female oppression, the roots of war, or the meaning of love, Anne is not bashful about giving her opinions, which she does in a language that is both entertaining and gripping. . . .

Anne was at her best, however, when analyzing herself, monitoring her inner states as closely as Yitzhak tracked the progress of the Soviet Army and Moshe watched for signs from God to save His people. Of all the diarists, Anne is by far the most introspective. "Now I look back at that Anne," she wrote on March 7, 1944, referring to an earlier Anne, "as an amusing, but very superficial girl, who has nothing to do with the Anne of today.". . .

COMPARING ANNE'S REFLECTIVE NATURE

Different people, different diaries. David, Yitzhak, Moshe, Éva, and Anne had different sets of parents, who made their homes in different parts of Europe. They differed in character, temperament, and interests. . . . Anne, Moshe, David, and Yitzhak were able to keep their diaries for a long time, but only in Anne is there noticeable internal growth and development, as she is the first to tell us.

Situation and place had a lot to do with that. . . . Unlike David, Éva, and Yitzhak, Anne was not immediately threatened and had plenty of time to think, and so could freely write and reflect on God, human nature, the place of women, male-female relations, family. When a minister speaking on Radio Orange, the voice of the Dutch government in exile, urged people to record their experiences for possible inclusion in a postwar collection, she got excited and sat down to polish her prose. She planned to publish a book based on her experiences in the hideout, using the diary she called Kitty as a source. In addition to the diary, she was writing short stories and thinking about placing one with a publisher under an assumed name.

What reading was to Yitzhak and God to Moshe, writing was to Anne—"the finest thing I have." Writing kept her going: "I can shake off everything if I write; my sorrows disappear, my courage is reborn. . . ." She used her diary as a confessional and poured into it all her "joys, sorrows, and contempt." "Anyone who doesn't write doesn't know how wonderful it is. . . ." Without it, she said, she would suffocate. It was as a writer that she envisaged her future. The diary was the first thing she packed when they moved to the annex. When burglars were mucking around in the warehouse and someone suggested burning the diary because it would incriminate them if they were caught, Anne burst out: "Not my diary; if my diary goes, I go with it!"

A PASSION FOR LEARNING AND SELF-IMPROVEMENT

Anne Frank shared with the other teenage writers a passion for learning. "The only way to take one's mind off it all is to study, and I do a lot of that." "Oh, something else, the Bible," she exclaimed on May 11, 1944, "how long is it going to take before I meet the bathing Suzannah? And what do they mean by the guilt of Sodom and Gomorrah? Oh, there is still such a terrible lot to find out and to learn." One day Anne had a "pile of work" to get through, which included finishing the first part of the biography of Galileo, copying and memorizing three pages of difficult vocabulary extracted from recent reading, working out the genealogies of members of the royal families found in the biography of Charles V she had just completed, and getting a handle on the Greeks Theseus, Oedipus, Peleus, Orpheus, Jason, and Hercules.

Anne considered herself a prime example of the human capacity for self-improvement. . . . Anne was totally focused and set high goals for herself. She dreamed of fame—"I want to go on living even after my death!"—and criticized her mother and Margot. Anne could not see herself as "merely a housewife." She yearned to go to Paris and London, learn the languages, study art history. She wanted to meet interesting people and wear nice dresses, and "a little money" wouldn't hurt, either. "Compare that with Margot, who wants to be a midwife in Palestine!" Anne vowed that she'd "work in the world and for mankind!" But unlike Yitzhak Rudashevski and Moshe Flinker, who made similar commitments, she did not say how.

Anne's breezy writing style and cheery disposition make it easy to forget that the "secret redoubt" was a pressure cooker bursting with tension. The lodgers quarreled, bombers roared, burglars prowled, and the specter of discovery hovered. "At night, when I'm in bed," Anne wrote on November 8, 1943, "I see myself alone in a dungeon, without Mummy and Daddy. Sometimes I wander by the roadside, or our 'Secret Annex' is on fire, or they come and take us away at night. I see everything as if it is actually taking place, and this gives me the feeling that it may all happen to me very soon!" She was well aware that the "little piece of blue heaven" that was the hiding place was under siege by "heavy black rain clouds" that were coming closer and closer and threatened to crush them. No wonder she took tranquilizers every day "against fear and depression."

REALITY OUTSIDE THE ANNEX

But the tension in the "house in back" was very different from that experienced by the young writers in Vilna, Nagyvárad, and Krajno. . . . In the Amsterdam refuge, persecution, destruction, and death were shadows hovering offstage.

Still, the news that penetrated the annex was horrible enough. The makeshift quarters that lay concealed at the top of the narrow stairs behind the fake bookcase had one great merit—its only merit: It kept the real world out, which, after all, was the whole point. The outside hardly entered, except as filtered through the "illegal" broadcasts of the BBC and Radio Orange in London and the small but devoted group of friends who looked after the Franks. What Anne learned about Westerbork, for example, made her tremble with fear. The human warehouse on the Dutch heath conjured up visions of the fate that would be hers, if discovered: cattle cars, shaved heads, prisoners dumped pell-mell in large barracks. "If it is as bad as this in Holland," she wrote in October 1942, "whatever will it be like in those distant and barbarous regions they are sent to? We assume that most of them are murdered. The English radio speaks of their being gassed.". . .

HOW ANNE COPED

But unlike, say, David or Yitzhak, Anne was in a position to avert her eyes, while her temperament, in contrast to Moshe's, enabled her to turn the horror off and to pull the blankets over her head. Anne felt it was no use to turn the hideout into a "Secret Annex of Gloom." "Must I keep thinking about those other people, whatever I am doing?" she asked herself, referring to the Jews who had been deported. "And if I want to laugh about something, should I stop myself quickly and feel ashamed that I am cheerful? Ought I then to cry the whole day long? No, that I can't do. Besides, in time this gloom will wear off." Having witnessed a procession of hungry and ill-clad children, she commented: "I could go on for hours about all the suffering the war has brought, but then I would only make myself more dejected." After hearing that Holland was to be emptied of Jews, province by province, she remarked: "These wretched people are sent to filthy slaughterhouses like a herd of sick, neglected cattle. But I won't talk about it, I only get nightmares from such thoughts.". . .

ANNE'S OPTIMISM AND VIEW OF EVIL

Anne had a sunny disposition. "I'm not rich in money or worldly goods, I'm not beautiful, intelligent, or smart," Anne wrote on March 25, 1944, "but I am and I shall be happy! I have a happy nature, I like people, I'm not distrustful and would like to see all of them happy with me."

Happiness and optimism go hand in hand. Anne's father's positive attitude seems to have rubbed off on his younger daughter. How can you get over feeling low? Think about all the misery in the world and count your lucky stars, Anne's mother advised. But Anne thought differently: "I don't see how Mummy's idea can be right, because then how are you supposed to behave if you go through the misery yourself? Then you are lost. On the contrary, I've found that there is always some beauty left—in nature, sunshine, freedom, in yourself; these can all help you. Look at these things, then you find yourself again, and God, and then you regain your balance. And whoever is happy will make others happy too. He who has courage and faith will never perish in misery!". . .

Anne saw her fellow human beings as capable of self-improvement through individual effort and of taking control over their own lives. Evil in Anne's view was an aberration, a temporary relapse into barbarism. . . .

We will never know whether Anne was able to hold on to her beliefs in Auschwitz and Bergen-Belsen.

Though the Nazis killed them all, Anne, David, Yitzhak, Moshe, and Éva left diaries that demonstrate the endurance and beauty of the human spirit—"in spite of everything." All five stand as a testimony and an inspiration, as if to urge us never to give up hope.

CHAPTER 2

ARREST AND ANNIHILATION

PEOPLE
WHO MADE
HISTORY

ANNE FRANK

The Arrest

Ernst Schnabel

In an effort to learn more about Anne Frank, author
Ernst Schnabel interviewed over forty of the Frank
family's friends and acquaintances, especially those
who remembered Anne. Schnabel collected these interviews and has written one of the most respected
books about Anne Frank, *Anne Frank: A Portrait in
Courage*. By utilizing these interviewees' memories,
Schnabel is able to movingly reconstruct many of the
pivotal moments in Anne's life, including her arrest.

   In this selection about the arrest of Anne and the
other members of the Secret Annex, Schnabel directly quotes the people who risked their lives to
hide the Franks. With these memories and details, he
provides the reader with a very personal and detailed account of the frightening moments as the office workers and those in hiding come to realize that
the police have finally come for them. Since Anne's
diary ends three days before this event, these interviews give the reader new insight into Anne's final
moments in hiding.

Henk [Gies] says: On August 4 I was again going my rounds.
As it approached noon I went to the Prinsengracht [the office
building where the Franks were hidden] to eat with [his
wife] Miep and the others. We always had lunch together,
you see.

   "I went to the building and up the stairs, but as I opened
the office door Miep rushed up to me and whispered
sharply: 'Gestapo!'

   "Just that one word. And as she said it she pressed her
purse with our money and ration cards into my hand, and I
gave her the bread I had brought and left quickly. There was
no one in the street, nor had I seen anyone in the building. I
reached my office safely. It was only seven minutes from the

Ernst Schnabel, *Anne Frank: A Portrait in Courage*, translated by Richard and Clara
Winston. New York: Harcourt, Brace, 1958. Copyright © 1958 by Harcourt, Inc. Reproduced by permission.

Prinsengracht, but I was glad when I arrived there. I took out everything I had in my pockets, the lists with the addresses of the strangers I was supposed to visit that day, put it all into my desk drawer, and locked the drawer. Then I considered for a moment, and then I went back to the Prinsengracht."

BUSINESS AS USUAL

What happened in the house on the Prinsengracht on that fourth of August, 1944, was far less dramatic than it is now depicted on the stage. In reality the automobiles did not approach with howling sirens, did not stop with screaming brakes in front of the house. The bell was not rung. No rifle butt rapped against the door till it reverberated as it now reverberates in the theater every night somewhere in the world. The truth was, at first no one heard a sound. *They* were practiced, skillful, and quiet in such cases.

Mr. [Jo] Koophuis says:

"It was a Friday, and a fine August day. The sun was shining; we were working in the big office, Miep, Elli [Vossen], and myself, and in the warehouse below us the spice mills were rumbling.

"When the sun was shining the trees along the canal and the water itself would often cast flecks of light on the ceiling and walls of the office, ripples of light that flickered and danced. It was an odd effect, but we knew then that it was fair outside."

Mr. Frank says:

"It was about half past ten. I was upstairs in the van Daan's part of the house, in Peter's room, doing schoolwork with him. Nothing could be heard. And if there really was anything to hear, I was at any rate not paying attention. I had just been giving Peter English dictation, and was saying to him: 'Why, Peter, you know that *double* is spelled with only one *b* in English.'"

THE POLICE ARRIVE

Elli says:

"Mr. Koophuis and Miep were writing and I was posting entries in the receipts book when a car drove up in front of the house. But cars often stopped, after all. Then the front door opened, and someone came up the stairs. I wondered who it could be. We often had callers. Only this time I could hear that there were several men. . . ."

Miep says:

"The footsteps moved along the corridor; then a door creaked, and a moment later the connecting door to Mr. Kraler's office opened, and a fat man thrust his head in and said in Dutch: 'Quiet. Stay in your seats.'

"I started, and at first did not know . . . but then I knew."

Mr. Koophuis continues:

"I suppose I did not hear them because of the rumbling of the mills downstairs. The fat man's head was the first thing I saw, and then the door opened a little farther and I saw that there was another man standing in front of [Victor] Kraler, asking him something. I think Kraler answered him. He was sitting at his desk, saying something, and then he rose slowly to his feet and went out with the man. I heard them on the stairs. There was nothing more he could do now.

"The fat man came in and planted himself in front of us. 'You three stay here, understand?' he barked.

"So we stayed in the office and listened as someone else went upstairs, and doors rattled, and then there were footsteps everywhere. They searched the whole building."

WHAT THE POLICE ALREADY KNEW

Mr. Kraler wrote this account:

"It was a very fine summer day. Suddenly a staff sergeant of the 'Green Police' and three Dutch civilians entered my office and asked me for the owner of the house. I gave them the name and address of our landlord. No, they said to me, we want the person who is in charge here. That is myself, I replied. Then, 'Come along,' they ordered.

"The police wanted to see the storerooms in the front part of the building, and I opened the doors for them. All will be well if they don't want to see anything else, I thought. But after the sergeant had looked at everything, he went out into the corridor, ordering me again to come along. At the end of the corridor they drew their revolvers all at once and the sergeant ordered me to push aside the bookcase at the head of the corridor and open the door behind it. I said: 'But there's only a bookcase there!' At that he turned nasty, for he knew everything. He took hold of the bookcase and pulled at it; it yielded and the secret door was exposed. Perhaps the hooks had not been properly fastened. They opened the door, and I had to precede them up the steps. The policemen followed me; I could feel their pistols in my back. But since the steps were only wide enough for a single person, I was the first to enter the Franks' room. Mrs. Frank was standing at the table. I made a great effort and managed to say: 'The Gestapo is here.'

"She did not start in fright, nor say anything in response."

THE ARREST BEGINS

Otto Frank continues:

"I was pointing out to Peter his mistakes in the dictation when someone suddenly came running up the stairs. The steps creaked, and I started to my feet, for it was morning when everyone had to be quiet—but then the door flew open and a man stood before us holding his pistol aimed at my chest. The man wore civilian clothes.

"Peter and I raised our hands. The man told us to step forward, and we had to walk past him, and then he ordered us to go downstairs, while he followed us with the pistol.

"Downstairs all the others were already assembled. My wife and the children and the van Daans were standing there with raised hands. Then [Alfred] Düssel [who was also in hiding] came in, followed by another stranger. In the middle of the room stood a 'green policeman.' He scrutinized our faces."

Miep later found out the name of this "green policeman." We will call him Silberthaler.

The witnesses all agree that he was a stocky man of medium height, middle-aged, and that his face was not unpleasant, not icy or cruel, at any rate. Miep says:

"He looked as though he might come around tomorrow to read your gas meter or punch your streetcar ticket."

THE "GREEN POLICE"

The "green policeman" was accompanied by four or five Dutch Nazis. They wore plain-clothes and were "eager beavers," behaving rather like the detectives in a movie thriller.

After the war Mr. Koophuis identified these men from an album of photographs shown to him by a war-crimes investigating commission. One of them, he said, was about fifty-five, the fat man about forty-five, the others somewhat younger. He told me that the Gestapo employed a great many such civilian agents. For the most part, they were men who were failures in life; there were criminals among them. But there were also some who had swallowed the Nazi line, and believed that what they were doing was good and right.

None of the occupants of the Secret Annexe had seriously counted on the possibility that they would be discovered.

MIEP GIES

Perhaps the most well known helper to the Frank family is Miep Gies. When the family went into hiding, Miep shared the secret, brought them food and special treats, and treated them like family. It was Miep who discovered Anne's diary and shared it with Otto Frank.

Of all the Jews for whom Amsterdam was a refuge—although only for a few short years—a talented adolescent named Anne Frank is perhaps the best known. Her diary, published after she died at 15 in the Bergen-Belsen camp, has given millions of readers a vivid look at a Jewish family's life in hiding during the German occupation of the Netherlands. Now, Miep Gies, one of the Christians who helped the Franks and others survive for 25 months in a secret annex, has told her side of the story in *Anne Frank Remembered*. . .

When Otto Frank confided to Miep Gies that he intended to hide his family behind the offices where she worked, she never hesitated. Not only would she keep the Franks' secret, she would help them all she could.

"We only did our duty," Gies, now 78, told *U.S. News* Senior Editor Alvin P. Sanoff. "So many people in Holland did the same work as we." She and Jan both worked very hard. Jan—called "Henk" in Anne's diary—secured forged ration tickets to cover the four Franks and three Van Daans who occupied the cramped office annex. Miep cultivated local grocers who tactfully ignored the large supplies of food she bought, then smuggled into the hideout. Every Saturday, she borrowed books for her charges. She always hoped to be able to throw open the door to the hiding place and announce: "We are free." Instead, she says sadly, "it was the Germans who came through the door."

In the end, Miep discovered Anne's diary in the mess left by the police who found the Franks and sent them off to the dreaded camps. She hid it away, unread, for Anne's return—and finally gave it to Otto, the sole Frank survivor, after they learned of Anne's death. To this day, she says, she and Jan find August 4—the date the Franks were arrested—"the bad-dest day in the year." They wait, silently, never looking at a clock until it is over, feeling only pain for their lost friends.

Alvin P. Sanoff, *U.S. News & World Report*, May 11, 1987.

The terrors they had suffered at the beginning, the terrors of those first nights, which each had had to bear by himself, were by now largely faded. Only Mr. van Daan had continued to have occasional fits of despair; he had once hinted to Mr. Frank that he could no longer endure life and that he would prefer the whole thing to be over, one way or another—he did not say precisely what he meant by this last phrase. But these crises were not due to premonitions of evil. He was worn out, while the others, the womenfolk, too, had become accustomed to the life they were leading.

Taken by Surprise

In recent weeks, however, even Mr. van Daan had been in good spirits. The war was clearly approaching an end. Every news report made that clear, even the German army communiqués. The Russians were well into Poland; in Italy the Allies had reached Florence. American forces had broken through at Avranches, and the armies landed in Normandy were pouring with tremendous power into the heart of France. At the moment a solid German western front no longer existed, and it looked as though no new one would be formed until Holland was liberated. Twenty-five months had passed since Anne had made her diary entry describing their arrival at the house on the Prinsengracht. Fear cannot be maintained for twenty-five months. They were now full of confidence. Only two months before, Anne had written:

Perhaps, Margot says, I may yet be able to go back to school in September or October.

And although such incidents as the burglary in April could still throw them into a fever of nervousness, their confidence had returned so quickly that Anne was able to describe the scene in almost comic terms:

I prepared myself for the return of the police, then we'd have to say that we were in hiding; they would either be good Dutch people, then we'd be saved, or N.S.B.-ers [Dutch Nazis], then we'd have to bribe them!

"In that case destroy the radio," sighed Mrs. van Daan. "Yes, in the stove!" replied her husband. "If they find us, then let them find the radio as well!"

"Then they will find Anne's diary," added Daddy. "Burn it then," suggested the most terrified member of the party. . . . "Not my diary; if my diary goes, I go with it!" But luckily Daddy didn't answer.

ALL THE VALUABLES, EXCEPT THE DIARY

"And now they stood before us," Mr. Frank says. "No, I had not imagined for so much as a moment what it would be like when they came. It was simply unthinkable. And now there they were.

"'Where is the storeroom?' they had asked downstairs. And now they asked: 'Where are your valuables?'

"I pointed to the cupboard where my cashbox was kept. The 'green policeman' took it out. Then he looked around and reached for Anne's brief case. He shook everything out, dumped the contents on the floor, so that Anne's papers and notebooks and loose sheets lay scattered all over the floor-boards. Then he put our valuables into the brief case, closed it, and asked us whether we had any weapons. But we had none, of course; anyway the plain-clothes men had already searched us thoroughly.

"Then he said: 'Get ready. All of you be back here in five minutes.'

"The van Daans went upstairs to fetch their knapsacks; Anne and Düssel went into their room, adjoining ours, and I reached for my knapsack, which hung on the wall. Suddenly the Gestapo man stopped in front of my wife's bed, stared down at the chest that stood between bed and window, and exclaimed: 'Where did you get this chest?'

A CHANGE IN ATTITUDE

"It was a gray foot-locker bound in iron, the kind we all had in the First War, and on the lid the words: 'Reserve Lieu-tenant Otto Frank.'

"'It is my own,' I said.

"'How come?'

"'I was an officer in the First War.'

"The man became exceedingly confused. He stared at me, and finally said:

"'Then why didn't you report your status?'

"I bit my lips.

"'Why, man, you would have been treated decently! You would have been sent to Theresienstadt.'

"I said nothing. Apparently he thought Theresienstadt a rest camp, so I said nothing. I merely looked at him. But he suddenly evaded my eyes, and all at once the perception came to me: Now he is standing at attention. Inwardly, this police sergeant has snapped to attention; if he dared, he might very well raise his hand to his cap in salute.

"Then he abruptly turned on his heel and raced upstairs. A moment later he came running down, and then he ran up again, and so he went, up and down, up and down, calling out: 'Take your time!'

"He shouted these same words to us and to his agents."

A Time to Wait

Mr. Kraler writes:

"They were all utterly calm. They did not wail and lament. There was not much time for lamentations, for they had to pack their things, and so none of them betrayed their real feelings,". . .

Koophuis says:

" . . . I said to Miep: 'Now you can go, too, Miep.' I pleaded with her to go, because there was no doubt about what they were going to do to us. But she would not leave."

Miep says:

"I couldn't leave. I think that was it: I simply couldn't go."

Koophuis:

"'You must know what you're about,' I said to Miep. 'At least take the office keys. Here they are. And do your best to steer clear of it. *You* can't save us. Save what still can be saved. Just deny everything, do you hear? First and foremost make sure you are not involved.'"

Miep:

"Mr. Koophuis gave me the keys to the office and I put them into my desk, but I just could not leave.". . .

Miep says:

"They must certainly have been in the building for at least an hour when one of the plain-clothes men came down, took a chair, and sat down in front of me, at my desk. He called some office and ordered a car sent over. 'But a big one!' he added. 'There are seven or eight of them.' The voice on the telephone answered something, and the man said Yes and Good. Then he left us alone again."

All Was Lost

Mr. Frank says:

"They gave us more time than we needed. We all knew what we had to pack—the same belongings we had planned on taking in case of fire.

"Once Anne came to me and I said: 'No, don't take that,

but you can take that along.' And she obeyed, for she was very quiet and composed, only just as dispirited as all the rest of us. Perhaps that was why she did not think to take along one of her notebooks, which lay scattered about on the floor. But perhaps, too, she had a premonition that all was lost now, everything, and so she walked back and forth and did not even glance at her diary.

"No one wept. It was just that all of us were terribly dispirited. None of us said a word more than was absolutely necessary. In any case these policemen had distributed themselves among the rooms and watched us while we packed. The Gestapo man could still be heard on the steps. And at last the van Daans came down. We were ready by then, too, and so we went out one after the other, through the open door. We left our hiding place, and went along the corridor and down the stairs. In the private office we had to wait again. Mr. Kraler was already there when we came in, and now Mr. Koophuis entered, and one of the agents took up a position between the two of them. The 'green policeman' wanted to interrogate them, but both of them stated they had nothing to say to him. At that he exclaimed:

"'All right, then you'll come along too.'"

THE FINAL MOMENTS AT THE ANNEX

Miep:

"And I heard them going, first in the corridor and then down the stairs; I could hear the heavy boots and the light footsteps, and then the very light footsteps of Anne. Through the years she had taught herself to walk so softly that you could hear her only if you knew what to listen for.

"I had seen her only the day before, and I was never to see her again, for the office door was closed as they all passed by."

Henk says:

"From my office I went back to the Prinsengracht, but I stayed on the other side of the canal, posted myself on the quay and looked across the water. After a while Mr. Koophuis's brother came and joined me. But we could not see what was going on inside the building, for while I had been away a big closed police van had driven up, and was parked so close to the door that we could not see who was coming out and going in."

Mr. Frank:

"Our two warehouse clerks stood in the front entry as we came down, M. and the other one, but I did not look as I passed them, and in memory I can only see their faces as pale, blank disks which did not move.". . .

Miep:

"I cannot say how late it was by now. I did not count the strokes of the bell, but it must have been noon. I stood behind the curtain, looking down at the street. The van had driven so close to the building that I had only a glimpse of the van Daans. They were deathly pale, but quite calm.". . .

MIEP IS SAVED

Miep says:

"Now I was alone in the building. I do not know whether the warehouse clerks were still downstairs in the storeroom. But I was alone upstairs, and after they drove off I sat down at my desk again and thought: Oh God. . . .

"After a while I heard footsteps on the stairs, and Silberthaler and one of the Dutch civilians came in. The civilian said:

"'Her? She was in on it, too. Sure.'

"I denied it.

"Then Silberthaler sent the Hollander out, and he planted himself in front of me and said: 'And what am I going to do with you?'

"He spoke in German, and I said: 'You're from Vienna, aren't you?'

"He was startled, so I said: 'I can tell from your speech. I am from Vienna, too.'

"When he asked for proof, I showed him my identity card. There it stood. He tossed the identity card onto the desk and exclaimed: 'And weren't you ashamed to help that Jewish trash?'

"I thought of what Mr. Koophuis had said, and replied: 'I knew nothing about it.'

"But he said: 'You did!' He insisted on it, and we argued back and forth, until I began to see that he didn't know what he ought to do with me. He picked up the identity card again, read it through once more, and then he slapped it violently down on the desk for the second time and said: 'I tell you what, I'm going to let you go. But just as a personal favor and for no other reason, do you hear? And you stay right here. You come to the office every day, as usual; then at least I'll know what you're doing. If you disappear we'll take your husband just like that, understand?'

"'My husband hasn't anything to do with the whole affair!'

"'Don't give me any of that. He knows perfectly well what has been going on.'

"He turned on his heel and left, slamming the door behind him so hard that the frosted glass rattled, and then he ran down the stairs. I went to the window and saw him coming out of the house with a bicycle. He wheeled it along for a short distance, because the Prinsengracht is a one-way street, but at the corner he mounted it and rode off.". . .

AT LEAST THEY KNEW

And Henk adds:

"I sat up half the night with Miep, and we discussed back and forth what, if anything, we could possibly do. We also called Mrs. Koophuis, but none of us had any ideas, and there was nothing more that we could do in the way of practical activity. I had already called on Mrs. Düssel, shortly after noon, in fact. She had suspected nothing, had not even known that her husband had been in Amsterdam all those two years, and so I told her. Now everyone concerned knew about it. At least they *knew*."

A Final Chance to See Her Friend

Alison Leslie Gold

Alison Leslie Gold has written several books on Anne Frank. After extensive interviews with Hannah Goslar, Gold shares the story of one of Anne's best friends, who Anne had called "Hanneli" or by her nickname "Lies" in her diary. Hannah and Anne had been best friends for nine years before Anne disappeared one day into hiding. Hannah believed that the Frank family fled to Switzerland, as Anne was not allowed to tell even her best friend where she was going. Hannah herself was arrested and sent to Bergen-Belsen concentration camp with her family.

In this article, Hannah was surprised to find that her friend Anne had not only been in hiding, but had been arrested and was in the camp with her. This selection shares a final meeting that the two best friends were able to have, through a barbed wire fence at the concentration camp, just days before Anne died of typhus. The piece ends with Hannah's memory of meeting Anne when they were small children, and finally of Anne's thirteenth birthday. Through these two memories, one in the camp just before Anne died, and the other just before she had even gone into hiding, the reader can catch a glimpse of how much Anne changed because of her experiences.

When February [1945] came Hannah had been in Bergen-Belsen a year. After work she would bend over the stove toward the small bit of heat and stretch her purple, frozen hands. When she had rubbed at the numbness, the sharp sting of pins and needles hurt her hands.

Mrs. Abrahams told Hannah that she had been right,

Alison Leslie Gold, *Memories of Anne Frank: Reflections of a Childhood Friend.* New York: Scholastic Press, 1997. Copyright © 1997 by Alison Leslie Gold. Reproduced by permission.

there were Dutch people on the other side of the fence. In fact, a woman there said that there was someone who knew Hannah.

Hannah summoned up her courage to risk the danger and, when it was dark, scurried over to the fence. Her breath billowed out in front of her. She prayed that the guard would not notice her there, that the searchlight would not pass across her. Am I crazy to risk everything by doing this? she asked herself and answered yes. But having human contact with someone Dutch would mean a great deal.

In Dutch she whispered softly into the barbed wire and straw.

A voice whispered back in Dutch. "Who are you?"

Hannah heard movement but could see nothing through the straw.

"It's Hannah Goslar from South Amsterdam."

She heard the voice say in Dutch, "Hanneli Goslar, it's me, Mrs. van Daan, the friend of the Frank family."

Hannah remembered Mrs. van Daan slightly. Her husband had worked with Mr. Frank at his office. Sometimes when her parents went to the Frank house for coffee and cake on Sunday afternoon, the van Daans and their son Peter had been among the guests.

"Do you know that your friend Anne is here?" Mrs. van Daan asked her.

Hannah couldn't have heard her right.

"Anne is in Switzerland."

"No. She's here. Do you want me to get her?" Mrs. van Daan asked.

"Oh! Yes!"

"I can't get Margot, she's very sick, but I'll get Anne."

HANNAH AND ANNE MEET AGAIN

Hannah prayed that the guard would not pass by. Her heart was pounding with elation. How could this be possible? She waited, excited but fearful all at once.

"Hanneli? It it really you?"

Of course it was Anne's voice.

"It's me! I'm here."

They began to cry.

"What are you doing here? You're supposed to be in Switzerland." Hannah asked.

Anne quickly told her that Switzerland was a ruse, that

they had wanted the Nazis to think they had fled to Switzerland, but really her family had gone into hiding.

Anne explained that they'd been hiding the whole time in a storage annex behind Mr. Frank's office on Prinsengracht. She told her that Miep Gies, who was their friend and also worked for Otto Frank, and a few other employees of her father, had looked after them for twenty-five months until they were arrested and deported.

For two years Anne had never stepped outside the hiding place, had not been allowed to write letters or contact anyone. They had had food and clothes. They were warm. It seemed like they would survive because the war was coming to an end, the Germans were losing.

Astonished, Hannah asked Anne if she knew for sure that the Germans were losing.

Anne assured her that it was true. Because they had had a radio in hiding, she was sure. On June 6, 1944, the Americans and British and Canadians had landed in France and had begun beating back the Germans. At the same time, in the East, the Russians had been pushing the Germans back. Then she told Hannah that her group in hiding were arrested in August and put in jail. Her family was sent to S barracks in Westerbork. In Westerbork Anne had worked at the battery factory.

THE FRIENDS HAVE GROWN UP

Hannah told Anne that she had been in Westerbork, too. Hannah remembered the shaved heads in S barracks in Westerbork. She remembered looking into the battery factory and seeing women at work. She realized that if Anne was much more grown up, she must be, too. It had been nearly two years since she'd seen herself in a mirror. Anne said Westerbork was hard but at least her family had been together.

Then, Anne told her emotionally, they were transported to Auschwitz, her father was taken away with the other men, things had gone from bad to worse for them since then. When she and Margot were shipped to Bergen-Belsen their mother had not been sent with them. She and Margot feared the worst for their parents. There were gas chambers in Auschwitz, Anne told her; night and day thousands of people were gassed and cremated.

Hannah was stunned by this information. Could it be possible? It must be; Anne had seen it with her own eyes.

Anne asked urgently about Hannah's parents.

Hannah told her that Mrs. Goslar had died in Amsterdam before they were arrested. So had the new baby. Grandfather had died in Westerbork. She explained that so far the rest of her family had managed to stay together—Gabi with her, Papa and Grandmother, all in the same camp but in different barracks. But now, she told Anne desolately, her father was in the hospital. He was very, very sick.

BROKEN GIRLS

"You're so lucky to have your family. I don't have parents anymore, Hanneli. I have nobody. Margot is very sick, too."

Again they began crying.

"They shaved my head."

Hannah thought, How terrible for Anne, she was so proud of her thick, lustrous hair.

The searchlight from the watchtower swept through the dark night. Hannah thought, Anne's not the same person. Neither am I. We're broken girls.

Desperately Anne revealed that she and Margot didn't have anything at all to eat in their compound. They were frozen and Margot was very sick. They'd been living in tents, but these had blown down. She also confided that they didn't have any wearable clothes since lice were in everything.

Hannah thought, Maybe I can scrounge up something for them. At least we have a little!

She asked Anne to meet her on the following night.

Anne reminded her how dangerous it was to talk to her, but said she would try to meet Hannah again.

HANNAH REMEMBERS MEETING ANNE

Lying beside Gabi, Hannah thought about the improbability of her reunion with Anne. She thanked God. Of course it was terrible that Anne was here and not in Switzerland. Hannah could barely believe what had actually just happened. When she thought over Anne's information that the war was coming to an end, that the Germans were losing, her spirits rose. Dare I hope that we will all go home? That Anne and I will walk to school together, maybe even this spring? she thought.

Her heart hammered with this miraculous possibility.

At age four, when they couldn't speak Dutch yet and wore little flowered dresses, Hannah and Anne had walked to school in the morning and home in the afternoon. At eight they'd ridden bicycles, at ten they'd gone swimming in summer and skating in winter, at twelve they'd played Ping-Pong and talked about the goings-on between boys and girls. . . .

CELEBRATING ANNE'S BIRTHDAY

On the day of Anne's last birthday, the twelfth of June in 1942, Hannah had kissed her parents and hurried down the street. It was Anne's thirteenth birthday. First she would pick her up, then they would walk together to school.

Like every day, at the door to Anne's brick apartment building, number 37 Merwedeplein, Hannah had whistled the two notes that signaled her arrival. The door had flown open, sending Anne almost into her arms and both of them into a cascade of giggles.

"You still have two left arms, Hanneli!" Anne had teased.

"*Hartelijk Gefeliciteerd*, Anne! Happy birthday, Anne!" Hannah wished her.

Anne had boasted that now Hannah couldn't tease her about only being twelve, while she was a mighty thirteen, since Hannah was six months older and had reached the grand old age of thirteen first. Anne was happy, her voice ringing.

That day the sitting room of the Frank apartment overflowed with flowers. Anne showed Hannah a blue blouse that her parents had given to her. She showed gifts from Margot, from Miep at her daddy's office, from Mr. and Mrs. van Daan, from Moortje her cat. They tasted chocolates from a box.

In Anne's bedroom were new games, books, a new red-checkered album, jewelry. Anne admitted that she was spoiled. Looking around, Hannah had seen that it was true. Anne was especially excited to own the red-checkered book that looked like an autograph album.

ANNE'S FAVORITE PRESENT

When Hannah asked if it was an autograph album, Anne explained that she was using it as a diary. Anne had been writing down her secret thoughts with her fountain pen, which had special gray-blue ink. But she never let any of her friends, even Hannah, read what she wrote. Anytime someone asked to see her private writing Anne would hide it with one hand and then tell the busybody, "It's none of your business!" in a flippant way. So, that morning, Hannah hadn't even asked to see what was inside.

After showing her new diary off, Anne had put it with her scrapbooks of cards of the children of kings and queens, and her collection of photos of movie stars. In the sitting room Mr. Frank sat in his favorite soft chair. Hannah liked Mr. Frank. He was lanky, balding, and read the *Joodse Weekblad* just as her own father did.

Mr. Frank had smiled his friendly smile at Hannah. He always made a little joke. Like her own father, Anne's father was no longer allowed to work in his firm in the old part of Amsterdam that produced products for jam and sausage making. Now he spent his days at home. But unlike Mr. Goslar, who was gloomy and pessimistic, Mr. Frank had a cheery disposition.

That day in the newspaper was the order that all Jews must hand in their bicycles by one P.M. on June 24. The bicycle must be in good working condition. Jews must not forget spare tires and tubes. Because thieves had stolen Anne's bicycle, and Mrs. Frank's bicycle and Margot's bike had been hidden, they would not have to hand anything in. It was exhilarating to put one over on the Nazis.

The smell of strong coffee always filled the sitting room. Hannah teased Anne by telling her that even though Anne was finally thirteen, Hannah would always be older. She was already thirteen and a half. When Anne's big eyes were showing their touches of green—a sure sign that Anne was angry—Hannah stopped teasing.

I Saw Anne Frank Die

Irma Sonnenberg Menkel

In 1997, Holocaust survivor Irma Sonnenberg Menkel turned one hundred. Fifty-two years earlier, she had been liberated from Bergen-Belsen concentration camp. Like Anne, Menkel's family fled from Germany to Holland to escape Nazi oppression in Germany. Also like Anne, she was caught and sent to Westerbork camp, and then moved to Bergen-Belsen. In this brief article from *Newsweek* magazine, Menkel shares memories of her time at Bergen-Belsen. Upon her arrival at the camp, she was placed in charge of one of the barracks. When Anne and her sister Margot arrived at Bergen-Belsen, they were assigned to Menkel's barracks. Though there were many children, Menkel remembers some small details about Anne, and tells of comforting Anne as she lay dying.

I turned 100 years old in April and had a beautiful birthday party surrounded by my grandchildren, great-grandchildren and other family members. I even danced a little. Willard Scott mentioned my name on television. But such a time is also for reflection. I decided to overcome my long reluctance to revisit terrible times. Older people must tell their stories. With the help of Jonathan Alter of *Newsweek*, here's a bit of mine:

I was born in Germany in 1897, got married and had two children in the 1920s. Then Hitler came to power, and like many other Jews, we fled to Holland. As the Nazis closed in, we sent one daughter abroad with relatives and the other into hiding with my sister and her children in The Hague. My husband and I could not hide so easily, and in 1941 we were sent first to Westerbork, a transit camp where we stayed about a year, and later to Bergen-Belsen, a work and transit camp, from where thousands of innocent people were sent to extermination camps. There were no ovens at Bergen-Belsen; instead the Nazis killed us with starvation and disease. My husband and brother both died there. I stayed for about three years before it was liberated in the spring of 1945. When I went in, I weighed more than 125 pounds. When I left, I weighed 78.

After I arrived at the Bergen-Belsen barracks, I was told I was to be the barracks leader. I said, "I'm not strong enough to be barracks leader." They said that would be disobeying a command. I was terrified of this order, but had no choice. It turned out that the Nazi commandant of the camp was from my home town in Germany and had studied with my uncle in Strasbourg. This coincidence probably helped save my life. He asked to talk to me privately and wanted to know what I had heard of my uncle. I said I wanted to leave Bergen-Belsen, maybe go to Palestine. The commandant said, "If I could help you, I would, but I would lose my head." About once every three weeks, he would ask to see me. I was always afraid. It was very dangerous. Jews were often shot over nothing. After the war, I heard he had committed suicide.

There were about 500 women and girls in my barracks. Conditions were extremely crowded and unsanitary. No heat at all. Every morning I had to get up at 5 and wake the rest. At 6 A.M., we went to roll call. Often we had to wait there for hours, no matter the weather. Most of the day, we worked as slave labor in the factory, making bullets for German soldiers. When we left Holland, I had taken only two changes of clothes, one toothbrush, no books or other possessions. Later I had a few more clothes, including a warm jacket, which came from someone who died. Men and women lined up for hours to wash their clothes in the few sinks. There were no showers in our barracks. And no bedding. The day was spent working and waiting. At 10 P.M., lights out. At midnight, the inspection came—three or four soldiers. I had to say everything was in good condition when, in fact, the conditions were beyond miserable. Then up again at 5 A.M.

One of the children in my barracks toward the end of the war was Anne Frank, whose diary became famous after her death. I didn't know her family beforehand, and I don't recall much about her, but I do remember her as a quiet child. When I heard later that she was 15 when she was in the camps, I was surprised. She seemed younger to me. Pen and paper were hard to find, but I have a memory of her writing a bit. Typhus was a terrible problem, especially for the children. Of 500 in my barracks, maybe 100 got it, and most of them died. Many others starved to death. When Anne Frank got sick with typhus, I remember telling her she could stay in the barracks—she didn't have to go to roll call.

There was so little to eat. In my early days there, we were each given one roll of bread for eight days, and we tore it up, piece by piece. One cup of black coffee a day and one cup of soup. And water. That was all. Later there was even less. When I asked the commandant for a little bit of gruel for the children's diet, he would sometimes give me some extra cereal. Anne Frank was among those who asked for cereal, but how could I find cereal for her? It was only for the little children, and only a little bit. The children died anyway. A couple of trained nurses were among the inmates, and they reported to me. In the evening, we tried to help the sickest. In the morning, it was part of my job to tell the soldiers how many had died the night before. Then they would throw the bodies on the fire.

I have a dim memory of Anne Frank speaking of her father. She was a nice, fine person. She would say to me, "Irma, I am very sick." I said, "No, you are not so sick." She wanted to be reassured that she wasn't. When she slipped into a coma, I took her in my arms. She didn't know that she was dying. She didn't know that she was so sick. You never know. At Bergen-Belsen, you did not have feelings anymore. You became paralyzed. In all the years since, I almost never talked about Bergen-Belsen. I couldn't. It was too much.

When the war was over, we went in a cattle truck to a place where we stole everything out of a house. I stole a pig, and we had a butcher who slaughtered it. Eating this—when we had eaten so little before—was bad for us. It made many even sicker. But you can't imagine how hungry we were. At the end, we had absolutely nothing to eat. I asked an American soldier holding a piece of bread if I could have a bite. He gave me the whole bread. That was really something for me.

When I got back to Holland, no one knew anything. I finally found a priest who had the address where my sister and daughter were. I didn't know if they were living or not. They were. They had been hidden by a man who worked for my brother. That was luck. I found them and began crying. I was so thin that at first they didn't recognize me.

There are many stories like mine, locked inside people for decades. Even my family heard only a little of this one until recently. Whatever stories you have in your family, tell them. It helps.

Anne's Last Seven Months

Willy Lindwer

Willy Lindwer is a Dutch filmmaker who won an International Emmy Award for his film documentary, *The Last Seven Months of Anne Frank*. In this documentary, Lindwer interviews six women who knew Anne during her final seven months, from her arrest in the Secret Annex to her death in Bergen-Belsen. He later compiled the complete text of these interviews into a book by the same title. This selection is from his interview with Janny Brandes-Brilleslijper.

Though Janny did not know Anne before her arrest, she first had contact with Anne and the Frank family as they were all waiting to be deported to Westerbork camp, the first stop for arrested Amsterdam Jews. This article begins at the train station as they are all waiting to travel to Westerbork. Janny later saw Anne in Auschwitz, and then finally in Bergen-Belsen, where she nursed Anne right before her death. It was Janny who wrote to the only survivor of the annex, Anne's father, Otto Frank, to inform him that both Anne and her sister Margot had died of typhus in Bergen-Belsen. Though Janny did not know Anne well, her experiences provide valuable insight into life in the concentration camps as Anne experienced it.

At the same time, another group of people arrived [for the Westerbork transport], among them Anne Frank and the Frank family. It struck me that the two girls were dressed in sporty clothes, with sweatsuits and backpacks, as if they were going on a winter vacation. The situation was somewhat unreal—the quiet of that morning and all those people being brought to the train.

The train had compartments closed off by doors on both sides. You stepped inside and then you sat there. I observed the girls attentively, but we didn't speak with each other during the trip.

When we arrived in Westerbork, we were terribly upset, for after all we didn't know where we were going. We saw each other again on the platform. That day, we were all interned in the "S" barracks (the punishment barracks)—the Frank family, too. We all had our own problems, of course. I found my sister again there, and my parents and my brother, and we didn't pay very much attention to what was going on around us. But still, a family like that, with two children. We knew that they were there, that they had been in hiding. What a shame to have been caught at the last minute. . . .

I know that my sister Lientje, especially, had contact with the mother of the girls, Edith Frank. The Frank girls were there, too. We sat at long tables while we split the batteries. There was talk, there was laughter. You kept your sorrow to yourself because you never talked about things of a more serious nature. You could never know whether you might not be endangering another person. . . .

Transported to Auschwitz

The Frank family was with us in the [cattle] car, but I only had contact with my sister. We protected each other against the shoving and the aggressiveness. The longer the trip lasted, the more belligerent people became. That's just the way it was. You couldn't get upset about that, because the kindest, gentlest people become aggressive when they've stood for a long time. And you get tired—so terribly tired—that you just want to lean against something, or if possible, even if only for a minute, to sit down on the straw. Then you sit on the straw and they step on you from all sides because you are sitting so low. All those feet and all that noise around you makes you aggressive—that goes without saying. And then you, too, push and hit. That's unavoidable, but Lientje tried to hold a small place clear for me and I tried to do the same for her. Near the bolts on the door, there was a hole through which you could look to see the landscape. If you were lucky enough to get a glimpse outside without being pushed away, you could breathe a little and put your thoughts in order.

By putting your thoughts in order, what I mean is that all

the time you are busy thinking: How can I keep my feet on the ground? Can I sit down now for just a minute? How am I going to get past these legs? Watch out that Lientje doesn't push against that man, or he'll punch her. We weren't the only people who had these thoughts. Through that hole, you could see the marvelous landscape; we rode through magnificent cornfields. Everything was so peaceful and the weather was so wonderful that you forgot for a moment that you were sitting in a cattle car and that a war was going on.

We didn't realize where the train was going. . . .

But standing on the loading platform in Auschwitz, we knew that we were in Poland.

We arrived in the dark. To start with, we went through the gates. The first thing we saw was the infamous sign: ARBEIT MACHT FREI. It was oppressively quiet. We passed many watchtowers, little houses surrounded by barbed wire, and high electric poles. Everyone knew immediately where we were. It was so insane—that moment of realization, Yes, this is an extermination camp. It was dreadful, horrible. . . .

We saw the Frank girls only briefly in Auschwitz. We weren't in the same barracks with them and we didn't come across them at work. We only met them again after the transport to Bergen-Belsen. . . .

On to Bergen-Belsen

In the final days of October, we were put on the transport to Bergen-Belsen.

In the beginning of November, we were called at roll call. They didn't say anything, but we sensed that something was going to happen. And it was true. They wanted to evacuate the camp because the Russians were getting closer. The camp was to be emptied, but we didn't know that. At the time we left Westerbork in cattle cars, we had had the feeling that we were being sacrificed, and so close before the liberation. And who would know where we had gone? After that, the hell of Auschwitz broke out all around us. And now we were in that hell and we were being transported again.

As far as we could see, it couldn't get any worse. Nothing could be worse than Auschwitz. We were picked out and told to go from one platform to the other, where we got bread and a few pots of water to take along. And then we were in the cattle cars again.

That trip lasted a terribly long time. There were air raid

alarms and our train was fired on because the English prob-ably thought it was a troop transport. And then the guards fled from the train, which we didn't know. We sat inside, and on the platforms we got fresh water and sometimes a piece of bread. We were allowed to go outside a couple of times; getting back on, you tried to be the last, in order to stay as close to the doors as possible. The two of us always tried to stay by the doors as much as possible. You could lie down in the straw along the sides so that you were protected on one side at least, and you could get some air through the crack.

We didn't know what was going on; we knew absolutely nothing. We had the feeling that we were aimlessly riding around. Until we stopped in Celle and a lot of people said, "Oh, we're going to Bergen-Belsen, now that's a good camp!" But disillusionment followed immediately. In the streaming rain and cold—oh, it was so cold—we had to walk. We stayed close together, two horse blankets over two thin girls. I can still see us walking those few kilometers from the Celle sta-tion to the Bergen-Belsen camp. We walked through the woods and breathed deeply . . . hmmm, woods, delightful. . . . We were surrounded by guards, and we passed the little town—the people saw us, us poor outcasts. No one lifted a finger to help us. And it rained and stormed and hailed.

Finding Anne and Margot at Bergen-Belsen

Finally, we arrived at the camp on a moor with a bush here and there, and we sat down on a small hill, two girls pressed close together. But then another gray shape appeared and we threw the blankets off and called, "Oh, you're here too." It was Anne and Margot.

I have always assumed that they arrived on the same transport. There was a long, endless line entering the camp, and we sat on a little sand hill, as close together as possible, the blankets up to our noses, and then we suddenly saw those two girls also wrapped in blankets, and we thought, Well, they've gone through the same things we have. And then you are completely happy because you see that they've made it.

At that moment there was only happiness. Only the hap-piness of seeing each other. And we stayed together until we went into the tents. We also found the Daniëls girls whom we knew from Westerbork.

Maybe it was a "sister complex" that attracted our attention to the Frank girls and also to the Daniëls sisters. Sisters or mothers and daughters always tried to stay together. At that very moment, that feeling of togetherness, of having made it, was theirs as well. We had sort of motherly feelings for them because they were ten years younger than we were. On that same transport, we also found Sonja Lopes Cardozo and the daughter of Greetje van Amstel. We were reunited with quite a few of the young people, but that one moment, sitting on that little hill, we felt real joy because the children were still there. Now we felt at home. We took care, somehow, to see that the children stayed near us.

HORRIBLE SLEEPING CONDITIONS FOR THE GIRLS

Large tents were put up hastily because, as we heard later, Bergen-Belsen had not counted on these transports at all. Beds were shoved into those army tents, one, two, three on top of each other. We were soaked and cold, and as soon as the tents were up, everyone ran to them. There was terrible elbowing and pushing to get inside the tents as quickly as possible. But we held back; at one point, the Frank girls were bickering about whether they should go in, and then they did.

We really weren't always nice to each other. Sometimes it almost came to blows. But the Frank girls decided to go on ahead of us. We waited a bit longer in the rain, and finally we were the very last ones to go into the tents. That was our usual strategy, and had been our salvation often. We had to scramble all the way to the top.

During the night there was a terrible storm, with thunder and lightning and hail and you name it—everything that the weather gods could produce came down on us and shook and tore at the tents. Two or three tents, including ours, collapsed.

In each tent, there were a couple of hundred people. A lot of people were injured and, I think, even a few died. We were fortunate. Because we had crept up high and the canvas was torn, we were able to get out. But there was terrible devastation. And in the morning, it was as if there had been a shipwreck. People and piles of wreckage everywhere—moaning and pain.

We didn't find the Frank girls until a few days later. We were transferred to wooden and stone barracks. We stayed the longest in the wooden barracks. Naturally, we went to look for people we knew. Not the Frank girls in particular, just acquaintances. We found quite a few, people with whom we had talked and had contacts, with whom we had been together, and with whom we once had a party, up on our bed in Auschwitz. . . .

Taking Care of Little Children

There was a large group of Dutch children there and the Nazis didn't know if they were Jewish or not. They might have been *Mischlingen* (children from mixed marriages) and questions might come up about them later. So the authorities took special care of those children.

All of us, especially the young women, would go to see the children regularly to tell them a few simple children's stories. Normally they heard only screaming *Aufseherinnen* (supervisors) and *Kapos*, who only wanted to further their own interests through the children. We clipped the nails and, once in awhile, the hair of the tiny one. We acted toward them like anxious mothers. Fortunately, the majority of the children were taken by the Red Cross to Eindhoven soon after the liberation. I've had word from some of them, but I lost sight of most of them. Besides, I think that most of the children didn't want any more contact because they wanted to forget as much as possible, and that is for the best.

I know that Anne and Margot also involved themselves with the children and that we did our best to help them. Not only Anne and Margot, but also the other girls we knew went regularly to provide them with a little balance and sometimes a little culture.

It is very important sometimes to disengage yourself from the mess in which you find yourself, to shut your eyes and turn yourself off. I have to say that I myself, when we were removing dead people's bodies, stood in front of that stinking pit many times and turned around and looked at that magnificent starry sky and said, "Oh God, if you really exist, how could you let this happen?". . .

As nurses, we had to count the sick people and report them during the *Zählappell;* we were now in a somewhat better position. In Auschwitz-Birkenau, they would go to the infirmary barracks, but in Bergen-Belsen, the infirmaries were so full that those who were ill stayed in their own barracks. Ours was this kind of barracks. We had our hands full, but we continued to look for acquaintances. Roosje Pinkhof was with us in the barracks and Carrie Vos, too. The Daniëls girls came to see us regularly.

THE REALITY AT BERGEN-BELSEN

I didn't visit the headstrong Frank girls very often. When we wanted to find them in that total chaos of Bergen-Belsen, we couldn't because their barracks had been moved. . . .

Because of our [nursing] duties, we had access to the SS pharmacy where we could surreptitiously steal things, like aspirin, salve against lice, and other medications. We distributed what we got, also to the Frank girls, who weren't in our barracks.

There was no gas chamber in Bergen-Belsen, at least not within our range. But there was an enormous pit and we dragged our dead there. I always have a little trouble with the word "corpse." I never think of a corpse as a dead human being.

Young girls who were still strong, such as Roosje and Carrie, and whoever else could, also carried dead people wrapped in blankets, to the pit. But we wanted to keep those blankets and, in a manner of speaking, they were shaken empty into that large, stinking pit. The smell was indescribable. And then the birds that flew down into it. . . .

ANNE AND MARGOT CONTRACT TYPHUS

Anne had typhus. I had typhus myself, but right up to the end, I was able to stay on my feet. I took only aspirin since I had a raging fever. There was too much to do. Lientje was sick. Water had to be fetched. I always tried to first make sure that Lientje had water; that wasn't egotistical, that was normal; I thought that I had the right to favor my sister. And in fact, I wouldn't have wanted to come back to Holland if my sister hadn't survived. Only on the day of liberation did I finally collapse. But up to then I kept myself on my feet, in spite of being sick.

Anne was sick, too, but she stayed on her feet until Margot died; only then did she give in to her illness. Like so many others, as soon as you lose your courage and your self-control. . . .

We did what we could, but there was no question of real nursing. The nursing only consisted of giving the sick some water to drink and, if you had the chance, washing them off a little. In the first place, the most we could do for people with open, gaping wounds was to use a paper bandage. There wasn't anything else, no nursing supplies. An awful lot of people had frostbite. When you stood, for hours, at the *Zäh-*

lappell, then there were black toes, noses, and ears—jet black.

The women who were ill, including the Frank sisters, were in the regular barracks, not in the infirmary barracks. They were once in the infirmary barracks, but then one got another of them out, just as we had done. Our help wasn't enough, but we couldn't do more than we did. Above all, Lientje was already sick then. I had, of course, told the children stories, and when Lientje was sick, I brought Brammetje and Jopie Assher to her and thought up games for them. Lientje did as much as I did, no mistake about it. But it was simply a battle. Mrs. Scheermes died in that barracks, with her baby—who was still alive—in her arms. Nursing gave us the opportunity to offer help to the Frank children, and to others as well.

ANNE'S LAST DAYS OF SICKNESS

At a certain moment in the final days, Anne stood in front of me, wrapped in a blanket. She didn't have any more tears. Oh, we hadn't had tears for a long time. And she told me that she had such a horror of the lice and fleas in her clothes and that she had thrown all of her clothes away. It was the middle of winter and she was wrapped in one blanket. I gathered up everything I could find to give her so that she was dressed again. We didn't have much to eat, and Lientje was terribly sick but I gave Anne some of our bread ration.

Terrible things happened. Two days later, I went to look for the girls. Both of them were dead!

First, Margot had fallen out of bed onto the stone floor. She couldn't get up anymore. Anne died a day later. We had lost all sense of time. It is possible that Anne lived a day longer. Three days before her death from typhus was when she had thrown away all of her clothes during dreadful hallucinations. I have already told about that. That happened just before the liberation. . . .

NOTIFYING OTTO FRANK

In those days, I also went immediately to the Red Cross to look at the lists that showed who had survived and who had died. And I put a cross next to the names of those who I knew had actually died.

I also put a cross next to the names of Anne and Margot. Much later, in the summer of 1945, a tall, thin, distinguished man stood on the sidewalk. He looked through our window and Bob [Janny's husband] opened the door, because he often protected me. In the beginning, I had to deal so much with family members whom I had to tell that their sons, daughters, and husbands would not be coming back. That was often unbearable. And it was especially difficult to deal with because I had survived and had come back.

And there stood Otto Frank. He asked if I knew what had happened to his two daughters. I knew, but it was hard to get the words out of my mouth. He had already heard from the Red Cross, but he wanted to have it confirmed. He had also been to see Lientje. Lientje, who had been terribly ill, had rented a small house in Laren. He had gone to Laren and spoken with Lientje and [her husband] Eberhard. And I had to tell him that . . . that his children were no more.

He took it very hard. He was a man who didn't show his feelings openly, he had tremendous self-control. He was a tall, thin, aristocratic man. Later, we saw him frequently. By a remarkable chance, Anne's manuscript (her diary) was found at Annie Romijn's. And Annie Romijn was in our circle of friends. That's really amazing. And later he came often. He always stayed at the Hotel Suisse on Kalverstraat, where my relatives from Brussels always stayed. I always found that so nice.

CHAPTER 3

ANNE FRANK, THE WRITER

PEOPLE WHO MADE HISTORY

ANNE FRANK

The Diary Found, Revised, Published, and Translated

Gerrold van der Stroom

Taken from an essay found in *The Diary of Anne Frank: The Critical Edition*, this piece traces the development of Anne's diary and writings into a series of published works. Gerrold van der Stroom is one of the editors of this comprehensive edition of the diary, which was prepared by the Netherlands State Institute for War Documentation.

Anne's father, Otto Frank, kept all the diaries and papers that were found in the annex after the family's arrest. This essay details how Frank began the process of compiling, editing, translating, and ultimately finding a publisher for his daughter's writings. Van der Stroom also describes the various stages of development as the diary was published for different audiences and in different times, ultimately becoming a book that is recognized throughout the world.

Anne Frank was thirteen years old on June 12, 1942. Among her presents was an album of the type used to collect autographs, nearly square in shape, with a red and white checked cover. She was to use it as her diary. On her birthday she wrote on the front page: "I hope I shall be able to confide in you completely, as I have never been able to do in anyone before, and I hope that you will be a great support and comfort to me." This album, to which we shall be referring as "Diary 1," covers the period from June 12 to December 5, 1942, although Anne Frank made some additions to it in 1943 and 1944 when she also used up some of the pages she had previously left blank.

"Daddy has tracked down another new diary for me" was

Gerrold van der Stroom, "The Diaries, Het Achterhuis and the Translations," *The Diary of Anne Frank: The Critical Edition*, edited by David Barnouw and Gerrold van der Stroom, translated by Arnold J. Pomerans and B.M. Mooyaart. New York: Doubleday, 1989. Copyright © 1989 by Gerrold van der Stroom. Reproduced by permission.

the first sentence Anne wrote in the next diary that has come down to us. This one, to which we shall be referring as "Diary 2," was an exercise book, begun on December 22, 1943, more than one year after the last entry in Diary 1. It seems unlikely that Anne should have failed to keep a diary during this interval, and we must take it that this portion (made up, perhaps, of more than one part) has been lost. Diary 2 continues until April 17, 1944.

In 1943 and at the beginning of 1944 she also wrote *Verhaaltjes en gebeurtenissen uit het Achterhuis (Tales and Events from the House Behind)*, many of which have been published in English translation as *Tales from the House Behind* (The World's Work [1913] Ltd., 1962), and later as *Tales from the Secret Annex* (New York: Doubleday & Company, Inc., 1983). The account book in which these tales were written down, and to which we shall be referring as *Tales*, has also come down to us.

On the first page of the last diary, "Diary 3"—another exercise book—we read: "Diary of Anne Frank. from 17 April 1944 to." No end date is given. Anne Frank wrote in this volume for the last time on August 1, 1944.

ANNE'S INCENTIVE TO REVISE HER DIARY

A good four months earlier, on March 28, 1944, Gerrit Bolkestein, Minister of Education, Art and Science in the Dutch government in London, had delivered the following address to the Dutch nation on Radio Oranje:

> History cannot be written on the basis of official decisions and documents alone. If our descendants are to understand fully what we as a nation have had to endure and overcome during these years, then what we really need are ordinary documents—a diary, letters from a worker in Germany, a collection of sermons given by a parson or a priest. Not until we succeed in bringing together vast quantities of this simple, everyday material will the picture of our struggle for freedom be painted in its full depth and glory.

To that end, a "national center"—the later Netherlands State Institute for War Documentation—would be set up "in which all the historical material covering these years will be collected, edited and published—a center that will publish source material and papers, in Dutch and in the other leading languages."

"Of course, they all made a rush at my diary immediately," Anne Frank wrote a day after this broadcast. And she continued: "Just imagine how interesting it would be if I were to publish a romance of the 'Secret Annexe.' The title alone would be enough to make people think it was a detective story."

A week later she wrote:

> I must work, so as not to be a fool, to get on, to become a journalist, because that's what I want! I know that I *can* write, a couple of my stories are good, my descriptions of the "Secret Annexe" are humorous, there's a lot in my diary that speaks, but—whether I have real talent remains to be seen. [. . .] I can shake off everything if I write; my sorrows disappear, my courage is reborn. But, and that is the great question, will I ever be able to write anything great [. . .]?

On May 11, 1944, she confided to her diary:

> You've known for a long time that my greatest wish is to become a journalist someday and later on a famous writer. Whether these leanings towards greatness (or insanity?) will ever materialize remains to be seen, but I certainly have the subjects in my mind. In any case, I want to publish a book entitled *Het Achterhuis* after the war. Whether I shall succeed or not, I cannot say, but my diary will be a great help.

And then, after "a great deal of reflection," she wrote on May 20 that she had started on *Het Achterhuis*. "In my head it's already as good as finished, although it won't go as quickly as that really, if it ever comes off at all."

She rewrote her first diaries on sheets of copy paper, to which we shall be referring as the "loose sheets." Thus a second version in her handwriting came about. She changed, rearranged, sometimes combined entries of various dates, expanded and abbreviated. In addition she drew up a list of name changes: "Anne [Frank]" became "Anne Robin," "v. Pels" became "v. Daan," "Pfeffer" became "Dussel," "Kleiman" became "Koophuis," "Kugler" became "Kraler," "Bep" became "Elly" and so on. She no doubt compiled this list with an eye to the eventual publication of her diary. All the vicissitudes of life in the Annexe in 1943 were described by her on the loose sheets, and there can be no doubt that at the time she must still have been in possession of the relevant part (or perhaps the relevant parts) of her first version. That version was therefore not lost until later. But her second version, also, has not come down to us in full. The last entry on the loose sheets records the events of March 29, 1944. Anne must have reached this point in her rewriting at the beginning of August 1944. It was on August 4 that the *Sicherheitsdienst* raided the Annexe.

MIEP GIES SAVES ANNE'S WRITINGS

On the afternoon of that fatal day, after the eight hidden Jews, together with Kleiman and Kugler, had been taken away, Miep Gies was left alone in the office while the two warehousemen were below. Wisely, Bep Voskuijl stayed away for the first few hours. She and Jan Gies came back at about five o'clock. With Miep and Van Maaren they then went up to the Annexe. According to Miep:

> They'd gone through all the cupboards. On the floor lay books, papers and whatever else was of no importance to the 'Green Police.' At one point we found some loose pieces of paper, an old account book and the exercise books which we had given to Anne when the checked diary was running out of space for her notes. We took the diary, the account book, the exercise books and all the loose pages away with us. But we didn't dare stay up there too long because we were afraid that the 'Green Police' might come back.

Miep locked the diaries and the loose sheets away in her office desk.

One or more weeks later the Annexe was cleared by the removal firm of Abraham Puls on German instructions. On that occasion Miep told Van Maaren to go and collect any pieces of paper covered with writing that might come to light during this operation and give them to her. This he did, and she locked away those sheets, too, in her desk.

Otto Frank returned, via Odessa and Marseilles, to Amsterdam on June 3, 1945. He went straight from the station to the home of Miep and Jan Gies, and he stayed with them for the next few years. He already knew then that his wife was dead, but hope still lingered for his two daughters. At the time, Miep had Anne's writings and papers under lock and key in her desk. At the end of July or the beginning of August, when the fate of Margot and Anne became known, Miep handed Anne's writings over to Otto Frank. He took them with him to his private office and stayed away "for a few hours."

OTTO FRANK BEGINS THE PROCESS AND MAKES CHANGES

When Otto Frank had read his younger daughter's album, exercise books, account book and loose sheets, he began to make a copy of them on the typewriter in his room in the Gieses' home. As he later explained, at the time he only copied "the essentials" for the benefit of relatives and friends.

He omitted whatever he felt would prove of no interest to them, together with passages that might offend living persons, or remarks about Anne's mother that "didn't concern anyone else." The rest he translated into German and sent to his mother, who knew no Dutch, in Basle, Switzerland. According to Otto Frank, this first copy was lost. However the Frank family still have in their possession a copy of Diary 1 that was probably typed later.

Next, Otto Frank typed out another copy, based on Anne's loose sheets, i.e., on her own second—and final—version. For this typescript (to which we shall be referring as "Typescript I") Otto Frank also selected from the album and the exercise books—that is, from the first version—those items which again struck him as "essential." Seeing that it was not granted to Anne to rewrite her experiences in the Annexe after March 29, 1944, on the loose sheets, Otto Frank had no option but to use the first version for that period. Finally he added four "events" Anne had recorded in her *Tales*, that is, in the account book.

Typescript I has been preserved and is in the possession of the Frank family. The family placed it at the disposal of the Netherlands State Institute for War Documentation for the duration of the investigation into the authenticity of the diaries.

On examining Typescript I, we see that it was indeed compiled from the loose sheets, supplemented with some items from the first version and some from the *Tales*. By far the largest number of pages are composed of pieces of paper pasted together; they contain passages from the second version, or—to a lesser extent—from the first. Clearly, Otto Frank typed out those items in the two versions he wanted to use, cut some out and then joined them up.

Now, while it is true that Anne's second version was his guide in this, he did not copy it blindly, which is not surprising in view of his scruples when preparing the first copy, now lost. Thus he omitted an entry about the home of one of Anne's girl friends (a "bear garden") and also a passage attacking the Van Pels family; again, he left out a number of remarks his dead daughter had made about his dead wife. At the same time he omitted some rather duller entries: a report about Anne's Ping-Pong club, for instance, which was indeed of little interest. . . .

Apparently Otto Frank did not feel altogether sure of his ground; thus he handed Typescript I to his old friend Albert

Cauvern, the husband of his former secretary Isa Cauvern. In 1945, Cauvern was a dramatist working for VARA (the workers' broadcasting channel). Frank asked him to "revise" the manuscript, or, as he put it many years later, "to check it for grammatical errors and to remove Germanisms, that is, to correct expressions my daughter had borrowed from the German language and which were therefore bad Dutch." And Cauvern did as he was asked. . . .

In the late 1950s the German magazine *Der Spiegel* alleged that Cauvern had made a number of deletions from Anne Frank's text. Even earlier, another German magazine, *Welt am Sonntag*, had written to him about this. His reply was that "at the time" he "made only the most essential corrections (typing errors and lapses in idiom, grammar and punctuation). And he continues: "As for me, I have not deleted a single passage." This is plausible in view of the fact that Typescript I was in any case Otto Frank's abbreviated version of Anne's manuscript, and there was no reason for Cauvern to have cut it further. The typescript produced by Otto Frank and corrected and altered by others was retyped into a fair copy by Isa Cauvern, probably at the beginning of 1946. The resulting new typescript we shall refer to as Typescript II. This too has come down to us and is in the possession of the Frank family, who put it at the disposal of the Netherlands State Institute for War Documentation for the duration of the investigation.

COPIES FOR FRIENDS

As we said earlier, Otto Frank's first wish was that a wider circle should read the "essential" parts of his daughter's diary. To that end he had copies of Typescript II made for friends and close acquaintances, "that is, for people who I [Otto Frank] believe would be interested in these notes, from which much that concerns our fate emerges."

Dr. Kurt Baschwitz, lecturer in, and later professor of, journalism and mass psychology at Amsterdam, was one who saw the typescript. Baschwitz had emigrated in 1933 from Hitler's Germany to the Netherlands and had met Otto Frank in Amsterdam. The two families were on regular visiting terms. Baschwitz, too, went into hiding during the war. Later, one of his daughters spent some time abroad, and on February 10, 1946, her father wrote to her:

I have just been reading the diary of Anne Frank, the younger daughter of our friend Frank. You must have known her. They were, as you know, in hiding for 2 years. The girl, 14 and then 15 years old, kept a diary which got past the Germans as if by a miracle. It is the most moving document about that time I know, and a literary masterpiece as well. It reveals the inner experiences of a maturing girl, her impressions in close confinement with her father—whom she loved dearly, her mother—with whom she clashed, her sister—whom she discovered to be a friend, with the other family that shared their hiding place, and with their son, with whom she began to fall in love. I think it ought to appear in print.

That idea turned out to be not quite as simple as it looked.

TRYING TO FIND A PUBLISHER

Otto Frank had read parts of his daughter's manuscript to his friend Dr. Werner Cahn, who had escaped from Germany to the Netherlands in 1934 and was later active in the Dutch publishing world. It made a "great impression" on Cahn and his wife, and Cahn said that he would try to find a publisher. Otto Frank himself had not thought of publishing the diary at that juncture. As it was, both Em. Querido's Uitgeverij, the Amsterdam publishers, and the Fischer Verlag in Germany turned him down.

Cahn then obtained a copy of Typescript II. He was by this time working as copy editor for the ENSIE—Encyclopedia, whose editor was the well-known Dutch historian, Dr. Jan Romein. Cahn also knew Dr. Romein's wife, Dr. Annie Romein-Verschoor. . . .

Cahn was anxious to hear Annie Romein's opinion of Anne Frank's writings and gave her his copy of Typescript II. Evidently she recognized its importance and seems, in her turn, to have looked for a publisher. . . .

It looked as if it was going to be impossible to find a publisher for the book.

Years later Jan Romein commented, in a film produced by Jan Vrijman, that Otto Frank had come to see his wife with "a typed manuscript" (probably Typescript II) and had asked her to help him find a publisher. Otto had probably been introduced or recommended by Cahn. Finding a publisher for Anne's writings was proving to be no easy task. In the end Annie Romein was able, as we have said, to do very little. Jan Romein read the manuscript and was so deeply impressed that he wrote an article about it. The article was published on April 3, 1946, in *Het Parool:*

A Child's Voice

By chance a diary written during the war years has come into my possession. The Netherlands State Institute for War Documentation already holds some two hundred similar diaries, but I should be very much surprised if there were another as lucid, as intelligent, and at the same time as natural. This one made me forget the present and its many calls to duty for a whole evening as I read it from beginning to end.

When I had finished it was nighttime, and I was astonished to find that the lights still worked, that we still had bread and tea, that I could hear no airplanes droning overhead and no pounding of army boots in the street—I had been so engrossed in my reading, so carried away back to that unreal world, now almost a year behind us.

It is written by a Jewish girl who was thirteen years old when she went into hiding with her parents and an older sister and began this diary, and it ends one wretched day more than two years later when the Gestapo discovered the family. One month before the Liberation she died in one of the worst German concentration camps, not yet sixteen.

How she died, I do not wish to ask; it was probably in much the same way as has been described in so many camp reminiscences, for instance in the recently published pamphlet "*Tusschen leven en dood in Auschwitz* [Between Life and Death in Auschwitz]," although that was a different camp.

The way she died is in any case not important. What matters far more is that her young life was willfully cut short by a system whose witless barbarity we swore never to forget or to forgive while it still raged, but which, now that it belongs to the past, we are already busily, if not forgiving, then forgetting, which ultimately comes to the same thing.

To me, however, this apparently inconsequential diary by a child, this "de profundis" stammered out in a child's voice, embodies all the hideousness of fascism, more so than all the evidence at Nuremberg put together. To me the fate of this Jewish girl epitomizes the worst crime perpetrated by everlastingly abominable minds. For the worst crime is not the destruction of life and culture as such—these could also fall victim to a culture-creating revolution—but the throttling of the sources of culture, the destruction of life and talent for the mere sake of mindless destructiveness.

If all the signs do not deceive me, this girl would have become a talented writer had she remained alive. Having arrived here at the age of four from Germany, she was able within ten years to write enviably pure and simple Dutch, and showed an insight into the failings of human nature—her own not excepted—so infallible that it would have astonished one in an adult, let alone in a child. At the same time she also highlighted the infinite possibilities of human nature, reflected in humor, tenderness and love, which are perhaps even more astonishing, and from which one might perhaps shrink, especially when they are applied to very intimate matters, were it not that rejection and acceptance remain so profoundly childlike.

That this girl could have been abducted and murdered proves to me that we have lost the fight against human bestiality. And for the same reason we shall lose it again, in whatever form inhumanity may reach out to us, if we are unable to put something positive in its place. The promise that we shall never forget or forgive is not enough. It is not even enough to keep that promise. Passive and negative rejection is too little, it is as nothing. Active and positive "total" democracy—politically, socially, economically and culturally—is the only solution; the building of a society in which talent is no longer destroyed, repressed and oppressed, but discovered, nurtured and assisted, wherever it may appear. And with all our good intentions, we are still as far from that democracy as we were before the war.

J. Romein

This article caused a stir. Various publishers approached Jan Romein, who referred them to Cahn. One was Uitgeverij Contact in Amsterdam. "I remember very clearly," said K. Lekkerkerker, then an editorial consultant at Contact, "coming into the office one morning with Jan Romein's article about Anne Frank. It must have been April 4, 1946, for the article had been published in *Het Parool* the day before." He gave it to F.E.A. Batten, another editorial consultant at Contact, and asked him to bring it to the attention of the managing director, G.P. de Neve. According to Lekkerkerker, De Neve too must have been impressed by Romein's article and Batten then contacted Cahn. Batten's enthusiasm persuaded Cahn to submit the typescript for consideration. Thus Typescript II found its way to Contact.

PUBLISHER AND CENSOR

Batten advised publication, but De Neve had reservations. The precise nature of these remains unclear, but it is probable that he entertained scruples about certain passages concerning Anne's sexual development. Thus we know that Otto Frank wrote in 1978 to C. Blom, former financial director of Contact, that he knew "that [Contact] had not wanted, among other things, to publish letters referring to sexual topics (menstruation).". . .

In other words, the copy which De Neve saw—Typescript II—which had been compiled by Otto Frank, contained passages that De Neve thought unsuitable or indecorous and accordingly left out. This agrees with what Batten wrote to the Amsterdam historian Dr. Richter Roegholt in 1979:

> "I know [. . .] that passages about Anne Frank's mother and Anne's account of her own development into adulthood were deleted from the text offered to Contact on option. These passages were still in the text handed to me by Werner Cahn, who at the time represented Mr. Frank in matters concerning the publication of Anne's book."

To this we should add that all omissions and changes had to be agreed to by Otto Frank, as Anne's heir. And this is indeed what happened, for in 1949 he declared:

> The text was edited at the request of the publishing house. Some unimportant changes were made with my agreement. In addition some passages were left out, again with my agreement. These were entries by my daughter which it was felt might cause offense to the readers. Thus, for instance, the penultimate paragraph of the Dutch version of the entry on January 5, 1944, was a slight abbreviation of the typescript and the original version, in that the story of the two girls touching each other's breasts was omitted; that passage, however, was included in the German edition without objection.

A MORE LITERARY WORK

. . . It is clear that the deletions in Typescript II were made by Contact. Otto Frank obviously saw no reason for omitting the relevant passages from his Typescript I, and for that reason they also appear in Typescript II, i.e., in the typescript handed to Contact. They were probably cut by Contact in order to make the book fit into their Prologue series. The deletion of several other passages was above all the result of the view—held especially by De Neve—that they offended against propriety. Otto Frank concurred. It is by no means unusual for a publisher to make changes, and that is what happened at Contact. As a result the reader was left with a literary work by Anne Frank rather than with an autobiographical document *sensu strictu* [in the strict sense].

The manuscript was now ready. Lekkerkerker took one more look at it and wrote on the title page: "ready for compositor, K[ees] L[ekkerkerker]." And so, in an edition of 1,500 copies, with a preface by Annie Romein-Verschoor and an extract from Jan Romein's article "A Child's Voice" on the jacket, Anne Frank's *Het Achterhuis. Dagboekbrieven van 12 juni 1942—1 augustus 1944* was published as part of the Prologue series in the summer of 1947. "BOOK," Otto Frank wrote in his own diary on June 25, 1947.

He had carried out his daughter's wish, and *Het Achterhuis* was its fulfillment. . . .

THE GERMAN TRANSLATOR

In 1946, meanwhile, a German translation of Typescript II had been made. This translation was originally intended for Anne's grandmother in Basle, who, after all, could not read Dutch, the translation previously done by Otto Frank of the earliest (lost) copy being apparently inadequate.

The journalist Anneliese Schutz, an acquaintance of Otto Frank, offered her services for the new translation. She came from Berlin, had also escaped to the Netherlands, and before the war she had taught Margot literature and had also known Anne. Otto Frank accepted her offer and she set to work. . . .

Anneliese Schutz did not prove to be the most suitable translator for Anne's work. "She was," Otto Frank admitted later, "too old for the job, many of her expressions were pedantic and not in a youthful enough style. In addition she [. . .] misunderstood many Dutch expressions.". . .

Nevertheless Otto Frank felt that "Frau Schutz's translation could by and large be called faithful and in the spirit of the original." According to Werner Cahn, the translation

> "although correct, did not always reflect the style of the young Anne Frank. That is, in any case, a particularly difficult thing to do. But this may well be the reason why well-intentioned German literary circles occasionally expressed doubts about the authenticity of the diary."

Since Anneliese Schutz translated a copy of the complete Typescript II, her translation is more comprehensive than the Dutch edition, which was based on a shortened version of Typescript II. Thus in the German edition one does indeed find references to Körner's comedies, to French irregular verbs, the tale "Kitty" (not deleted until later), the vacuum cleaner, the touching of each other's breasts, the passages about menstruation, and so on. On the other hand, in Schutz's version, too, the St. Nicholas Day poems and the reference to Jo van Ammers-Küller have been omitted; they were probably thought to be incomprehensible to non-Dutch readers. . . .

In addition some changes were made of a more "political" nature. The explanation that to those listening to the radio in the Annexe "there were no forbidden stations with the proviso that it was understood that only exceptionally could one listen to German stations, for instance to hear classical music and the like," was omitted from the German version. The Dutch sentence "he ended up looking like a giant and he was the worst fascist there was" was shortened in German to "watching him grow into an invincible giant." The Dutch: "And indeed, there is no greater hostility than exists between Germans and Jews," became in German: "And there is no greater hostility in the world than between *these* Germans and Jews!" This change was agreed to by Otto Frank and Anneliese Schutz on the grounds that it reflected what Anne had actually wanted to say, since Anne,

> who despite the great tribulations she had suffered as a result of the persecution of the Jews and which she felt so acutely despite her youth, by no means measured all Germans by the same yardstick. For, as she knew so well, even in those days we had many good friends among the Germans.

The rule that people in the Annexe were required "to speak softly at all times, in any civilized language, therefore not in German," became in translation: "*Alle Kultursprachen . . . aber leise*!!! [All civilized languages . . . but softly!!!]." According to Otto Frank, this change was made by the German publisher. However, since it occurs in all four copies Otto must have been mistaken on this point. In addition "heroism in the war or when confronting the Germans" became in the German translation "heroism in the war and in the struggle against oppression.". . .

FINDING A GERMAN PUBLISHER

In short, in her translation of the Dutch version into German, Anneliese Schutz made mistakes, amplified—with or without consulting Otto Frank—and omitted references to the everyday speech of the Germans in hiding in the Netherlands lest German readers took offense.

That she did this last because, according to *Der Spiegel*, she believed that "a book intended after all for sale in Germany [. . .] cannot abuse the Germans" makes it likely that even while the translation was being undertaken it was planned to publish Anne's writings in German. In view of the negative attitude of Dutch publishers this need not surprise us.

Nevertheless it was not until 1950—by which time the Dutch edition was already in its sixth impression—that a German publisher, the Lambert Schneider Verlag in Heidelberg, agreed to add Anneliese Schutz's translation of Typescript II to its list. It appeared under the title *Das Tagebuch der Anne Frank*. The edition ran to about 4,500 copies. It sold moderately well. . . .

TROUBLE PUBLISHING THE DIARY IN ENGLISH

The English edition, on the other hand, had a more complicated history.

In November 1950, Vallentine, Mitchell & Co. Ltd. of London asked Mrs. B.M. Mooyaart-Doubleday to translate *Het Achterhuis*, and even before her translation was ready, Doubleday & Company, Inc., of New York had bought the U.S. rights.

In July 1951, Otto Frank called on the offices of Vallentine, Mitchell & Co. and handed them

> the text of those passages in the original Dutch typescript [= Typescript II] which were not printed in the Dutch edition because they were either too long, or were likely to offend Dutch Puritan or Catholic susceptibilities. [. . .] We think the English edition definitely ought to contain them, and wonder whether you would be so good as to translate them for us.

Thus wrote Vallentine, Mitchell to Mrs. Mooyaart. A month later she sent her translation of the extra passages to Vallentine, Mitchell. "So your long labour is really completed," the latter replied. "Today [August 17, 1951], the last batch went on to America. Everyone feels, who has read it, that it is going to be a wonderful book. Some passages go on moving me so deeply, though I've read them four or five times now."

As far as the later sections were concerned, the publishers wrote that "nearly all of it will go in."

In 1952, *The Diary of a Young Girl* by Anne Frank appeared in England as well as in the United States, where it had previously been rejected by some ten publishers. Both editions contained seven passages more than the Dutch, among them the letters of August 3, 1943, and April 15, 1944, about the mutual touching of breasts, menstruation and Franz Liszt. In addition we find the sentence "The Germans have a means of making people talk" inserted in the letter of May 22, 1944. No Dutch equivalent can be found in the typescripts that have come down to us or in the extant manuscripts. The origin of this phrase therefore remains obscure.

PUBLISHED THROUGHOUT THE ENTIRE WORLD

The Netherlands, West Germany, France, Britain and the United States were followed by East Germany, Switzerland, Italy, Denmark, Sweden, Norway, Finland, Iceland, Spain, Argentina, Mexico, Uruguay, Portugal, Brazil, Greece, Turkey, Hungary, Poland, Rumania, the Soviet Union, Czechoslovakia, Yugoslavia, Japan, Israel, India, South Korea, Thailand, Nationalist China, South Africa, Indonesia and Bulgaria.

Anne Frank had posthumously captured the world.

Her triumphal progress has since taken on unprecedented proportions. Between fifteen and sixteen million copies of the book have been sold so far. In 1955 it was turned into a play in the United States and in 1957 a film was made. Both film and play were international successes. These achievements stimulated the sale of the book in the Netherlands; *Het Achterhuis* had not been reprinted since 1950, but in 1955 three editions rolled off the presses; there were three more in 1956 and nine in 1957. This renewed Dutch interest thus came about "via an international detour." In 1957, too, the Anne Frank Foundation was established for the purpose of "maintaining the premises at 263, Prinsengracht, Amsterdam, and especially the attached Annexe, as well as implementing the ideals bequeathed to the world in the Diary of Anne Frank." Almost half a million people visit the Annexe every year. Schools and streets have been named after Anne Frank throughout the world. For countless people she has become a symbol of the six million Jews murdered by the Nazis, but as Ed van Thijn, Mayor of Amsterdam, put it, in an address in English:

> not a symbol in an abstract sense, far away from reality: no, she is a symbol because she reflects reality, because she was just a girl of fourteen, fifteen years old.

She made the incomprehensible story of the Second World War comprehensible.

She brought abstract statistics down to a human level; and everybody understands that the story of the Second World War is the story of six million individual human tragedies, six million dramatic personal life stories at least.

Anne's Talent as an Author

Mirjam Pressler

German writer Mirjam Pressler is an expert on Anne Frank. She has translated the Dutch edition of the diary into German, and she is the coeditor, with Otto Frank, of the "Definitive Edition" of the diary. In her book, *Anne Frank: A Hidden Life*, Pressler provides a straightforward presentation of Anne's life and her diaries. In this selection, Pressler concentrates not on memories of Anne, but rather on Anne's abilities as a writer by examining Anne's writing itself—both the diary and the short stories she produced during her two years in hiding. Pressler points out that for Anne, "writing was not lonely"; rather it was a way for her to have a best friend and a means to deal with life in hiding. Anne clearly wanted to be a professional writer, as is evidenced by her revisions and the methods she used in compiling her diaries. Pressler's analysis shows that Anne had the talent and the discipline to become the writer that she dreamed of becoming.

I have read all I could find about Anne Frank, including accounts by people who knew her or followed her trail, and I have spent a long time working on her diaries. Has it brought me any closer to her? Perhaps. But I don't want to rely too heavily on speculation. In what I say about her, I want to be guided mainly by what she wrote herself. The girl Anne is dead, but the writer Anne Frank will live on as long as she finds readers. I am therefore beginning Anne Frank's story with her work as a writer; here we have the diaries, the stories, all in black and white, although of course this is only one aspect of Anne as a person, only one piece of the truth.

Mirjam Pressler, *Anne Frank: A Hidden Life*, translated by Anthea Bell. New York: Dutton Children's Books, 1999. Copyright © 1999 by Macmillan Children's Books. Reproduced by permission.

MORE THAN A PLACE FOR SECRETS

What made this girl write? She wanted to keep a diary, but that is not unusual in adolescent girls, and teenagers of her time probably kept diaries more often than teenagers today. So there is nothing out of the ordinary about a girl sitting at a desk, leaning over the paper, blushing as she confides her secrets to her diary. However, it is obvious that Anne Frank wanted more than just a safe place for her secrets. She enjoyed writing for its own sake; it was a way to depict herself—a way to paint a verbal picture of herself and her place in the world.

An early example is the story of the essay Anne had to write as a punishment, set by a teacher because she had been talking in class. She describes it on Sunday, June 21, 1942, not long after beginning her diary.

> He assigned me extra homework. An essay on the subject "A Chatterbox." A chatterbox, what can you write about that? [. . .] I began thinking about the subject while chewing the tip of my fountain pen. Anyone could ramble on and leave big spaces between the words, but the trick was to come up with convincing arguments to prove the necessity of talking. I thought and thought, and suddenly I had an idea. I wrote the three pages Mr. Keesing had assigned me and was satisfied. I argued that talking is a female trait and that I would do my best to keep it under control, but that I would never be able to cure myself of the habit, since my mother talked as much as I did, if not more, and that there's not much you can do about inherited traits.

This little incident shows that Anne Frank enjoyed writing and found it a challenge. She tended to write well-rounded stories with a beginning, a middle, and an end, and it cannot be just because of her interesting situation that there are not many unfocused emotional outpourings in her diaries but a relatively large number of self-contained scenes where she shows her ability to confine herself to essential details. She never gave in to the obvious temptation for someone in her difficult position to write in an exaggerated way.

OBSESSED WITH WRITING

However, that still does not explain her growing passion for writing. Later on, it became almost an obsession. If she had simply liked narrative, writing for its own sake, she would have concentrated more on the stories she wrote for *Tales from the Secret Annex*. But even after August 1943, when she had begun writing stories and was feeling very enthusiastic about them, she did not neglect her diary. We cannot know how much she really wrote at this time, since version A, her original diary, is not preserved for the period between December 5, 1942, and December 22, 1943, but she did not abandon the diary in favor of the stories; in fact, the entries for 1944 are particularly long. Where did she get this passion for what is, after all, a very lonely pursuit?

The reason is fairly obvious: for her, writing was not lonely at all. Anne made her diary into a person; she made it "you," someone to talk to, "Kitty," the real friend she had wanted for so long. It was an extremely "literary" approach to adopt. Many children think up imaginary friends on whom they project their wishes and longings, but they do not very often make the imaginary friend into a literary character. However, this isn't exactly true. "Kitty" never really becomes a character in Anne Frank's writing. We hear hardly anything about her; instead, she enables Anne Frank to become a literary character herself. This shows that Anne could assess her gift even if her grasp of it may have been intuitive, for she always wrote best when she kept close to real life and the interpretation of real life. Her purely fictional stories are rather leisurely and wordy by comparison.

Her diary entry of June 20, 1942, in which she writes of her wish for a girlfriend and her decision to make the diary that friend, comes from version B, the one she was planning for publication; that is to say, it was really written not in 1942 but in the spring of 1944, by way of background information for her eventual readers. *Since no one would understand a word of my stories to Kitty if I were to plunge right in, I'd better provide a brief sketch of my life, much as I dislike doing so.* (There is no need for a background sketch of the writer's life in a private diary not intended for publication; at most the diarist may refer briefly to it.) In version B, Anne Frank explains why her diary entries take the form of letters: *To enhance the image of this long-awaited friend in my imagination, I don't want to jot down the facts in this diary the way most people would do, but I want the diary to be my friend, and I'm going to call this friend Kitty.*

HOW SHE DEVELOPED HER DIARY

In fact, the creation of Kitty took quite a long time. The entry for June 15, 1942, in version A of the diary contains considerably less on the subject of Anne's imaginary friend: *Jacqueline van Maarsen is supposedly my best friend, but I've never had a real friend.* Anne decided on the form her diary would take on September 21, 1942, when she says in version A (quoted here from the Critical Edition)

> I would just love to correspond with somebody, so that is what I intend to do in future with my diary. I shall write it from now on in letter form, which actually comes to the same thing.

> Dear Jettje, (I shall simply say), My dear friend, both in future as well as now I shall have a lot to tell you. [. . .] Regards to everyone and kisses from Anne Frank

So at this point her correspondent is Jettje, not Kitty. However, the two names are connected because they come from the same book. Anne Frank twice mentions the children's writer Cissy van Marxveldt (1893–1948), who was extremely popular in the Netherlands at the time. On September 21, 1942, she notes: *Every other week Mr. Kleiman brings me a couple of books written for girls my age. I'm enthusiastic about the* Joop ter Heul *series. I've enjoyed all of Cissy van Marxveldt's books very much. I've read* The Zaniest Summer *four times, and the ludicrous situations still make me laugh.* And on October 14, 1942, she adds: *Cissy van Marxveldt is a terrific writer. I'm definitely going to let my own children read her books too.*

The *Joop ter Heul* series, named for its heroine, has five books in all. It follows the fortunes of a "club" of girls from school to marriage and motherhood. The subjects of the books are not very different from those of the girls' books published elsewhere in the world at the same time—stories with an almost educational feel to them, preparing girls for their future roles as wives and mothers. In style, however, they are quite different—more colloquial and amusing; it is tempting to say more modern. The first book in the series, although lightweight by today's standards, is particularly pleasant and easy to read, and we may safely assume that Cissy van Marxveldt had some influence on Anne Frank's own style. In any case, the names of the girls are interesting: Joop, Pop (Emilie), Phien (Philipiene), Marjan, Lou, Connie, Jettje, and—Kitty Francken. They are all members of the club and were Anne Frank's first correspondents. . . .

   She decided on Kitty as her correspondent, and her letters to the others became less and less frequent; the last is dated

November 13, 1942, and addressed to "Jetty." Anne Frank incorporated it into version B, dated November 12, 1942, but this time it is addressed to Kitty. Of course, we cannot know if there were any more letters to other members of the club. At some point, however, Anne Frank came to the decision to write only to Kitty, who had become *her* friend, and the other girls are not mentioned in version B. It may have been Kitty's similar last name, Francken, that made her Anne's choice. All Anne's longing for friendship and communication was now concentrated on Kitty.

A Desire to Communicate

However, even this original way of coping with her need for intimacy and company would not in itself make Anne Frank a writer. To be a writer, you must have the desire (and of course the ability) to portray yourself, giving form to your life, your ideas, and your needs, intensifying them so that you can put them down on paper. Anne Frank's mastery of that ability, despite her youth, must surely have been partly due to her situation. Her world had to be small enough to fit into the Secret Annex, its few rooms, the hallway, and the attic. The immediate surroundings of the Annex, which offered a little variety, at least at first, were confined to the firm's offices, and Anne could only occasionally look out at the world beyond through a crack in the curtains. The few people she saw through binoculars or walking along the street had to replace not only the whole city but also school, outings, trips, everything. Her only glimpse of natural beauty consisted of the leaves and flower spikes of the chestnut tree outside the window, a few clouds passing by, a seagull. She could make a forest out of a leaf, the whole wide world out of a drifting cloud. She created nature inside her head; a little moonlight now and then aroused her romantic feelings—and what really made her a writer was this ability to create wide-ranging emotions out of relatively small incidents and then describe them.

Equally important, however, was her wish to communicate with other people, people she did not know: this led to her decision to copy out her diary and adapt it for publication, which showed strong creative will. Anne Frank frequently read through and revised the second version of the diaries, and indeed the first. She corrected spelling mistakes, crossed out words and replaced them with others, and generally polished her writing. By the time she wrote the second version of her diary, Anne Frank was no longer just a young girl writing a diary, but a real writer with the clear intention of writing literature. We can get an idea of the extent of her concentration on literary form from the fact that she made more than 2,900 changes and corrections in all (taking the diaries and the loose sheets together). They included many corrections of spelling mistakes, but a number of changes to style and content as well. In a girl of her age, such concentrated revision shows not only creativity but also a good deal of objectivity and self-criticism.

WOULD ANNE HAVE BECOME A WRITER?

It is pointless to wonder whether Anne would have become a writer if she could have lived her young life in normal circumstances, rather than in danger and in hiding. No one can say. Perhaps she would still have been a writer since she had abilities looking for expression, but the process would probably have taken longer. Perhaps she would not; she might have flung herself into life and all its pleasures instead of writing. As it was, however, while Anne the young girl had only a few square yards to live in, Anne the writer was embarking on the great adventure of her life with a fountain pen and some paper.

If I sound emotional here, it is because Anne Frank's story is so powerful. I have to be careful, though, not to idealize her too much or make her out to be very different from her many companions in misfortune. She was a writer but also a Jewish girl, one of many, and her existence and its extinction echoed those of other victims who never became famous. It is important to remember that she lived and died as one among millions of individuals; that must not be forgotten in our admiration for her diary.

Reading the Diary as Literature

Hedda Rosner Kopf

Hedda Rosner Kopf is an English professor and scholar whose focus is women writers. In this piece, Kopf examines the unique nature of Anne Frank's diary as literature. Though most diaries are personal and historical documents, Anne's diary is unique in that it goes beyond the traditional form of a personal diary. Literature is written for an audience, while a diary is often meant to be a personal account. Anne's diary began as a place for her to reveal her deepest thoughts, but after many months in hiding, she began to use her diary and the revisions she wrote as a way of practicing her skills as a writer.

In her desire to be a "famous writer" someday, Anne incorporated within her diary the literary elements of well-developed characters, carefully written descriptions of events and places, and purposeful revisions to produce a literary work. Recognizing these literary elements, Kopf encourages the study of the diary not only as an excellent example of a personal, historical record, but also as true literature.

Unlike memoirs and autobiographies which recollect and report at some later time in the subject's life, a diary records events and feelings as they are happening to the writer or very shortly after they occur. Therefore, the diary is a more immediate and often more accurate account of events and the writer's responses to them. Diary entries, however, do not have the benefit of the writer's understanding of how those events were resolved or what they would come to mean in the writer's life. For the most part, diary entries are made up of the raw material of the self.

Many diaries, especially those written by men before the nineteenth century, were meant to record the public lives of

Hedda Rosner Kopf, "The Diary as Literature," *Understanding Anne Frank's* The Diary of a Young Girl. Westport, CT: Greenwood Press, 1997. Copyright © 1997 by Hedda Rosner Kopf. Reproduced by permission.

their subjects, and therefore were written with a large audience in mind. Diarists often wrote with the intention of leaving behind a chronicle of their accomplishments for posterity.

Since the nineteenth century, the diary has evolved into a more personal account of the self, and often is written with the expectation that its contents will remain a secret. Many diarists write about subjects they are unwilling to share with others, and so the diary becomes a record of the diarist's most intimate and honest thoughts. At the same time, the diary is always a constructed text, and its author continually makes choices about what to include, leave out, emphasize, and repeat. Most of all, the diary is a work in process. Unlike the writer of the memoir or autobiography, the diarist never knows for sure what the next chapter will be about. Instead, the subject of the diary unfolds with each new day and moves toward an unknown future that the writer observes, records, and responds to within the private pages of the diary.

ANNE FRANK'S DIARY

Anne Frank's diary combines the elements of a public document with those of the outpourings of hidden feelings and thoughts. It is a factual document about the effects of the Holocaust on a young girl and her family, but it is also a chronicle of an adolescent's psychological and spiritual development. Anne began her diary as a private relationship between herself and her imaginary friend Kitty. Yet, as the months in hiding accumulated and she began to recognize the incredible circumstances under which she continued to write, Anne Frank consciously began to shape her diary into a public document as well. She thought about her intended audience, readers after the war, and she paid careful attention to the information she provided about the conditions she and the others endured.

Although her diary tells us about what happens to a real person, it also has many of the elements of the finest works of fiction: fully developed characters, vivid and acutely observed scenes, careful attention to language, and increasing suspense about the fate of the protagonist and the other seven Jews hidden with her in the secret annex. Above all, like all great literature, the diary has a "voice"—a distinct and vivid storyteller who speaks openly about her most private feelings and who endears herself to us as we get to know her fears, her joys, her anger, her dreams.

Anne received a red and white checked diary for her thirteenth birthday on June 12, 1942. In the first entry she listed a number of other birthday presents, but she tells her diary that the first gift *"to greet me was you, possibly the nicest of all."* Her second entry is dated June 20, 1942. During the week that elapsed between the first and second entries, Anne thought about what form her diary should take and what its purpose would be. She decided that she wanted her diary to be a place where she could *"bring out all kinds of things that lie buried deep in my heart."* Although Anne had a loving family and knew many people *"whom one might call friends,"* she did not feel that there was anyone in her life to whom she could reveal herself fully.

The diary would be the friend "Kitty" to whom Anne could tell everything. It also became a mirror in which Anne could see her own reflection more objectively. Fortunately for readers of Anne's diary, the "letters" she wrote required her to include information that her friend Kitty did not know. Thus, we learn about daily life in the annex as well as about the private thoughts and feelings Anne wanted to share with Kitty.

Writing to Kitty assumed a sympathetic "reader," a friend for whom Anne had *"waited so long."* Anne felt safe to tell Kitty everything, even the unpleasant truths about herself and her family. She could whine, complain, and have temper tantrums because her friend would accept and forgive her inadequacies in a way that Anne did not believe her family and friends would. Most of all, Kitty was *"patient"* with Anne, in contrast to the grown-ups, who constantly scolded her for her cheekiness and high spirits.

There is a particularly poignant aspect to the letters Anne wrote in her diary, because they did not reach anyone (although eventually, after her death, they reached across the entire world). Also, Anne never got a response to her beautifully written messages. Perhaps in choosing the letter form Anne was unconsciously insisting on keeping herself connected to the world beyond the secret annex, a world where mail was delivered and answered, and where a young girl's life mattered to someone.

PRACTICING HER CRAFT

Anne used her diary as a place where she could practice her writing skills, both because she found it easier to express herself on paper than through speech, and, more important, because she hoped to become "*a journalist someday and later a famous writer.*" Her diary was her apprenticeship, or what she refers to over and over again as her "*work.*" Deprived of her normal work life—school—Anne created a focus for the countless silent hours, days, weeks, and months during which she was trapped in the annex by writing her letters to Kitty.

Anne's literary ambitions for her diary were fortified when she heard a Dutch News radio broadcast from London in which a Dutch official said "*they ought to make a collection of diaries and letters after the war*" (March 29, 1944). Inspired by visions of her diary being published, Anne began rewriting and editing it. She went back to earlier letters to Kitty and revised them, adding details, changing words, or rearranging the order of her material. This process validated her image of herself as a writer, as someone who works at her craft. It also gave her a reason to go back and think about what she had written in terms of both its content and its style.

ANNE'S REVISIONS

A vivid example of Anne's process of revision is her entry on January 12, 1944. The first version reads:

> Isn't it odd, Kitty, that sometimes I look at myself through someone else's eyes? I see quite keenly then how things are with Anne Frank.

Her revised version reads:

> I have an odd way of sometimes, as it were, being able to see myself through someone else's eyes. Then I view the affairs of a certain Anne Robin at my ease, and browse through the pages of her life as if she were a stranger.

Although the inherent meaning of the two entries is similar, the changes suggest how thoughtful Anne was about her writing. For example, in the first version she asks Kitty, "*Isn't it odd . . . ?*" as if she needs Kitty's opinion or agreement on the matter. In the second version she simply states how she is "*able to see myself through someone else's eyes.*" She takes responsibility for describing herself without depending on Kitty's support. Interestingly, Anne changes her name to Anne Robin, an indication that she was thinking of her writing as material that might be published in the future under a pseudonym. She also made a list of pseudonyms for the other inhabitants of the secret annex for the same reason. The Van Pels family became the Van Daans, and Fritz Pfeffer became Alfred Dussel.

Finally, the second version is much more "literary." Anne uses language that connects her feelings of looking at herself *"through someone else's eyes"* with the idea of being a character in a book. She adds, *"I view the affairs . . . and browse through the pages of her life as if she were a stranger."* In fact, this is just what Anne did as she reread her diary entries and analyzed them objectively both as a young girl who was changing psychologically and as a writer who was improving her skills and nurturing her talent.

PUBLICATION OF *THE DIARY OF A YOUNG GIRL*

After his liberation from Auschwitz in January 1945, Otto Frank made his way back to Switzerland to see his mother and to recuperate from his ordeal in the concentration camp. He returned to Amsterdam in June 1945, hoping to find his daughters alive. He already knew that his wife had perished in Auschwitz, but he tried to be optimistic about the fates of Margot and Anne, who had been young and relatively healthy when they were transferred from Auschwitz to Bergen-Belsen, a labor camp. Otto Frank immediately went to Miep and Henk Gies and lived with them while he tried to find news of his daughters. After many inquiries, he finally received a letter from a nurse who had also been an inmate in Bergen-Belsen. She verified that Margot and Anne had died in the "Schonungsblock no. 19 in Bergen-Belsen prison camp."

Only after Anne's death had been confirmed did Miep give Anne's diary and her other papers to Otto Frank. She herself had never read Anne's private writings, but she had fervently hoped to return them to her young friend when she returned after the war. Instead, Otto Frank now had the enormous pleasure and pain of discovering his daughter's private joys and fears. Over the next several weeks Otto Frank translated sections of Anne's diary into German and sent them to his mother in Switzerland. Later, he transcribed the several versions of Anne's diary, editing out sections he thought might offend living persons or that he found too critical of his wife. Eventually, Otto Frank's manuscript of Anne's diary reached a prominent Dutch historian who was so impressed with the remarkable diary that he wrote an article about it for an Amsterdam newspaper. On

April 3, 1946, *Het Parool* printed "A Child's Voice," in which the historian declared:

> To me the fate of this Jewish girl epitomizes the worst crime perpetrated by everlastingly abominable minds. For the worst crime is not the destruction of life and culture as such . . . but the throttling of the sources of culture, the destruction of life and talent for the mere sake of mindless destructiveness.
>
> If all signs do not deceive me, this girl would have become a talented writer had she remained alive.

With this review, Anne Frank's diary became the subject of much interest. An edition of 1,500 copies was published as *Het Achterhuis* (The Secret Annex) in June 1947, and by 1950 the book was in its sixth printing in Holland. It was soon published in Germany and France, and the English version appeared in the United States in 1952. Although Anne's *Diary* had been turned down by a dozen publishers who did not believe people would be interested in reading about the sufferings of a young girl during World War II, the book was an immediate success. Its popularity continues; more than 25 million copies in fifty-five languages have been sold all over the world. . . .

USING THE DIFFERENT VERSIONS AS LITERATURE

While all of the diary versions tell Anne's story, readers can use the different versions now available as tools for reading Anne Frank's text as literature. The different translations and editions confirm the importance of language and style in Anne's writing and provide readers with vivid examples of the varying effects of word choice and syntax.

At the conclusion of her April 14, 1944 letter to Kitty, Anne writes, "'*The unbosomings of an ugly duckling' will be the title of all this nonsense. My diary really won't be much use to Messrs Bolkenstein or Gerbrandy*" (members of the wartime Dutch Cabinet-in-Exile in London, which planned to publish diaries and letters after the war). The diary is, in fact, a remarkably useful document for students of the Holocaust. Readers of Anne's diary can come to know the absolute depravity and horror of the Nazis' "Final Solution to the Jewish Question" by trying to understand what was lost with each death. Since it is impossible to comprehend the loss of 6 million voices, it is in contemplating the loss of Anne Frank's voice, only one voice, that we can begin to confront the endless abyss of that event.

Anne's diary does not take the place of history books and documents that explain what happened politically during World War II. Nor does her diary describe the unimaginable atrocities that Anne herself would see and suffer in Auschwitz-Birkenau and Bergen-Belsen. Nevertheless, everything she wrote about happened to her as a direct result of the Nazis' intention to implement the "Final Solution." We must acknowledge that *The Diary of a Young Girl* is about the effects of the Holocaust when we try to imagine how different her diary would have been if Anne Frank had lived in freedom and safety.

CHAPTER 4

ANNE FRANK'S LEGACY

ANNE FRANK

Who Owns Anne Frank?

Cynthia Ozick

Cynthia Ozick has been called one of the most important American writers of our day. She is noteworthy not only because of her award-winning skills as a fiction author, but also because her works, both fiction and nonfiction, focus predominately on issues of Judaism and the Holocaust. This article, written for *The New Yorker* magazine in 1997, is extremely insightful and controversial, as it causes the reader to see Anne's diary and her life in the light of the reality of Anne's ultimate death. Ozick reminds her audience that, despite the optimistic and heartwarming feelings that most people experience in reading the diary and watching the play adaptation, it is important to remember that in reality Anne died an untimely and inhumane death. Hers should be a tragic, not uplifting, story. Because Anne did not live to publish her diary herself, what the reader reads or the audience member views has been edited by those who, Ozick claims, had reasons to leave out controversial, discouraging, or unflattering material. To demonstrate her view, she points out that Otto Frank (Anne's father) often chose to exclude from the first edition of the diary sections which he believed to be contentious, such as Anne's thoughts on her family, religion, her body, or her views of the Germans. Ozick asserts that the stage play version of the diary in particular has been washed clean of the reality of Anne's existence, as a Jew, as a girl in hiding, and as an innocent victim of the Holocaust.

Ozick's final statement—that perhaps it would have been better if the diary had not survived—is not something she genuinely wishes, but demonstrates the depth of her belief that the real story of Anne Frank has been "sold out" by those who market her. Whether the reader agrees or disagrees with Ozick's main points, she raises questions that one should ask while reading and studying Anne Frank's life, including the title for her piece, "Who Owns Anne Frank?" Equally important are those questions she raises about the importance of representing Anne's life and the Holocaust accurately, and whether there is value in an incorrect or only partial reading of the diary.

If Anne Frank had not perished in the criminal malevolence of Bergen-Belsen early in 1945, she would have marked her sixty-eighth birthday last June [1997]. And even if she had not kept the extraordinary diary through which we know her it is likely that we would number her among the famous of this century—though perhaps not so dramatically as we do now. She was born to be a writer. At thirteen, she felt her power; at fifteen, she was in command of it. It is easy to imagine—had she been allowed to live—a long row of novels and essays spilling from her fluent and ripening pen. We can be certain (as certain as one can be of anything hypothetical) that her mature prose would today be noted for its wit and acuity. . . . "I want to go on living even after my death!" she exclaimed in the spring of 1944.

This was more than an exaggerated adolescent flourish. She had already intuited what greatness in literature might mean, and she clearly sensed the force of what lay under her hand in the pages of her diary: a conscious literary record of frightened lives in daily peril; an explosive document aimed directly at the future. In her last months, she was assiduously polishing phrases and editing passages with an eye to postwar publication. *Het Achterhuis*, as she called her manuscript, in Dutch—"the house behind," often translated as "the secret annex"—was hardly intended to be Anne Frank's last word; it was conceived as the forerunner work of a professional woman of letters.

Yet any projection of Anne Frank as a contemporary figure is an unholy speculation: it tampers with history, with reality, with deadly truth. "When I write," she confided, "I can shake off all my cares. My sorrow disappears, my spirits are revived!" But she could not shake off her capture and annihilation, and there are no diary entries to register and memorialize the snuffing of her spirit. Anne Frank was discovered, seized, and deported; she and her mother and sister and millions of others were extinguished in a program calculated to assure the cruelest and most demonically inventive human degradation. The atrocities she endured were ruthlessly and purposefully devised, from indexing by tattoo through systematic starvation to factory-efficient murder. She was designated to be erased from the living, to leave no grave, no sign, no physical trace of any kind. Her fault—her crime—was having been born a Jew, and as such she was classified among those who had no right to exist: not as a subject people, not as an inferior breed, not even as usable slaves. The military and civilian apparatus of an entire society was organized to obliterate her as a contaminant, in the way of a noxious and repellent insect. Zyklon B, the lethal fumigant poured into the gas chambers, was, pointedly, a roach poison.

Anne Frank escaped gassing. One month before liberation, not yet sixteen, she died of typhus fever, an acute infectious disease carried by lice. The precise date of her death has never been determined. She and her sister, Margot, were among three thousand six hundred and fifty-nine women transported by cattle car from Auschwitz to the merciless conditions of Bergen-Belsen, a barren tract of mud. In a cold, wet autumn, they suffered through nights on flooded straw in overcrowded tents, without light, surrounded by latrine ditches, until a violent hail storm tore away what had passed for shelter. Weakened by brutality, chaos, and hunger, fifty thousand men and women—insufficiently clothed, tormented by lice—succumbed, many to the typhus epidemic.

Anne Frank's final diary entry, written on August 1, 1944, ends introspectively—a meditation on a struggle for moral transcendence set down in a mood of wistful gloom. It speaks of "turning my heart inside out, the bad part on the outside and the good part on the inside," and of "trying to find a way to become what I'd like to be and what I could be if . . . if only there were no other people in the world." Those curiously self-subduing ellipses are the diarist's own; they are more than merely a literary effect—they signify a child's muffled bleat against confinement, the last whimper of a prisoner in a cage. Her circumscribed world had a population of eleven—the three Dutch protectors who came and went, supplying the necessities of life, and the eight in hiding: the van Daans, their son Peter, Albert Dussel, and the four Franks. Five months earlier, on May 26, 1944, she had railed against the stress of living invisibly—a tension never relieved, she asserted, "not once in the two years we've been here. How much longer will this increasingly oppressive, unbearable weight press down on us?" And, several paragraphs on, "What will we do if we're . . . no, I mustn't write that down. But the question won't let itself be pushed to the back of my mind today; on the contrary, all the fear I've ever felt is looming before me in all its horror. . . . I've asked myself again and again whether it wouldn't have been better if we hadn't gone into hiding, if we were dead now and didn't have to go through this misery. . . . Let something happened soon. . . . Nothing can be more crushing than this anxiety. Let the end come, however cruel." And on April 11, 1944: "We are Jews in chains."

The diary is not a genial document, despite its author's often vividly satiric exposure of what she shrewdly saw as "the comical side of life in hiding." Its reputation for uplift is, to say it plainly, nonsensical. Anne Frank's written narrative, moreover, is not the story of Anne Frank, and never has been. That the diary is miraculous, a self-aware work of youthful genius, is not in question. Variety of pace and tone, insightful humor, insupportable suspense, adolescent love pangs and disappointments, sexual curiosity, moments of terror, moments of elation, flights of idealism and prayer and psychological acumen—all these elements of mind and feeling and skill brilliantly enliven its pages. There is, besides, a startlingly precocious comprehension of the progress of the war on all fronts. The survival of the little group in hiding is crucially linked to the timing of the Allied invasion. Overhead the bombers, roaring to their destinations, make the house quake; sometimes the bombs fall terrifyingly close. All in all, the diary is a chronicle of trepidation, turmoil, alarm. Even its report of quieter periods of reading and study express the hush of imprisonment. Meals are boiled lettuce and rotted potatoes; flushing the single toilet is forbidden for ten hours at a time. There is shooting at night. Betrayal and arrest always threaten. Anxiety and immobility rule. It is a story of fear.

ONLY PART OF THE TRUTH

But the diary in itself, richly crammed though it is with incident and passion, cannot count as Anne Frank's story. A story may not be said to be a story if the end is missing. And because the end is missing, the story of Anne Frank in the fifty years since *The Diary of a Young Girl* was first published has been bowdlerized, distorted, transmuted, traduced, reduced; it has been infantilized, Americanized, homogenized, sentimentalized; falsified, kitschified, and, in fact, blatantly and arrogantly denied. Among the falsifiers have been dramatists and directors, translators and litigators, Anne Frank's own father, and even—or especially—the public, both readers and theatregoers, all over the world. A deeply truth-telling work has been turned into an instrument of partial truth, surrogate truth, or anti-truth. The pure has been made impure—sometimes in the name of the reverse. Almost every hand that has approached the diary with the well-meaning intention of publicizing it has contributed to the subversion of history.

The diary is taken to be a Holocaust document; that is overridingly what it is not. Nearly every edition—and there have been innumerable editions—is emblazoned with words like "a song to life" or "a poignant delight in the infinite human spirit." Such characterizations rise up in the bitter perfume of mockery. A song to life? The diary is incomplete, truncated, broken off—or, rather, it is completed by Westerbork (the hellish transit camp in Holland from which Dutch Jews were deported), and by Auschwitz, and by the fatal winds of Bergen-Belsen. It is here, and not in the "secret annex," that the crimes we have come to call the Holocaust were enacted. Our entry into those crimes begins with columns of numbers: the meticulous lists of deportations, in handsome bookkeepers' handwriting, starkly set down in German "transport books." From these columns—headed, like goods for export, *"Ausgangs-Transporte nach dem Osten"* (outgoing shipments to the east)—it is possible to learn that Anne Frank and the others were moved to Auschwitz on the night of September 6, 1944, in a collection of a thousand and nineteen *Stücke* (or "pieces," another commodities term). That same night, five hundred and forty-nine persons were gassed, including one from the Frank group (the father of Peter van Daan) and every child under fifteen. Anne, at fifteen, and seventeen-year-old Margot were spared, apparently for labor. The end of October, from the twentieth to the twenty-eighth, saw the gassing of more than six thousand human beings within two hours of their arrival, including a thousand boys eighteen and under. In December, two thousand and ninety-three female prisoners perished from starvation and exhaustion, in the women's camp; early in January, Edith Frank expired.

WHAT THE DIARY LEAVES OUT

But Soviet forces were hurtling toward Auschwitz, and in November the order went out to conceal all evidences of gassing and to blow up the crematoria. Tens of thousands of inmates, debilitated and already near extinction, were driven out in bitter cold on death marches. Many were shot. In an evacuation that occurred either on October 28th or on November 2nd, Anne and Margot were dispatched to Bergen-Belsen. Margot was the first to succumb. A survivor recalled that she fell dead to the ground from the wooden slab on which she lay, eaten by lice, and that Anne, heartbroken and skeletal, naked under a bit of rag, died a day or two later. . . .

The litany of blurbs—"a lasting testament to the indestructible nobility of the human spirit," "an everlasting source of courage and inspiration"—is no more substantial than any other display of self-delusion. The success—the triumph—of Bergen-Belsen was precisely that it blotted out the possibility of courage, that it proved to be a lasting testament to the human spirit's easy destructibility. *"Hier ist kein Warum,"* a guard at Auschwitz warned: here there is no "why," neither question nor answer, only the dark of unreason. Anne Frank's story, truthfully told, is unredeemed and unredeemable.

These are notions that are hard to swallow—so they have not been swallowed. There are some, bored beyond toleration and callous enough to admit it, who are sick of hearing—yet again!—about depredations fifty years gone. "These old events," one of these fellows may complain, "can rake you over only so much. If I'm going to be lashed, I might as well save my skin for more recent troubles in the world." (I quote from a private letter from a distinguished author.) The more common response respectfully discharges an obligation to pity: it is dutiful. Or it is sometimes less than dutiful. It is sometimes frivolous, or indifferent, or presumptuous. But what even the most exemplary sympathies are likely to evade is the implacable recognition that Auschwitz and Bergen-Belsen, however sacramentally prodded, can never yield light.

THE DIARY CAUSES MORE PROBLEMS

The vehicle that has most powerfully accomplished this almost universal obtuseness is Anne Frank's diary. In celebrating Anne Frank's years in the secret annex, the nature and meaning of her death has been, in effect, forestalled. The diary's keen lens is helplessly opaque to the diarist's explicit doom—and this opacity, replicated in young readers in particular, has led to shamelessness.

It is the shamelessness of appropriation. Who owns Anne Frank? The children of the world, say the sentimentalists. A case in point is the astonishing correspondence, published in 1995 under the title "Love, Otto," between Cara Wilson, a Californian born in 1944, and Otto Frank, the father of Anne Frank. Wilson, then twelve-year-old Cara Weiss, was invited by Twentieth Century Fox to audition for the part of Anne in a projected film version of the diary. "I didn't get the part," the middle-aged Wilson writes, "but by now I had found a whole new world. Anne Frank's diary, which I read and reread, spoke to me and my dilemmas, my anxieties, my secret passions. She felt the way I did . . . I identified so strongly with this eloquent girl of my own age, that I now think I sort of became her in my own mind." And on what similarities does Wilson rest her acute sense of identification with a hunted child in hiding?

> I was miserable being me. . . . I was on the brink of that awful abyss of teenagedom and I, too, needed someone to talk to. . . . (Ironically, Anne, too, expressed a longing for more attention from her father.) . . . Dad's whole life was a series of meetings. At home, he was too tired or too frustrated to unload on. I had something else in common with Anne. We both had to share with sisters who were prettier and smarter than we felt we were. . . . despite the monumental differences in our situations, to this day I feel that Anne helped me get through the teens with a sense of inner focus. She spoke for me. She was strong for me. She had so much hope when I was ready to call it quits.

A sampling of Wilson's concerns as she matured appears in the interstices of her exchanges with Otto Frank, which, remarkably, date from 1959 until his death, in 1980. For instance: "The year was 1968—etched in my mind. I can't ever forget it. Otis Redding was 'Sittin' on the Dock of the Bay' . . . while we hummed along to 'Hey Jude' by the Beatles." "In 1973–74," she reports, "I was wearing headbands, pukka-shell necklaces, and American Indian anything. Tattoos were a rage"—but enough. Tattoos were the rage, she neglects to recall, in Auschwitz; and of the Auschwitz survivor who was her patient correspondent for more than two decades, Wilson remarks, "Well, what choice did the poor man have? Whenever an attack of 'I-can't-take-this-any-longer' would hit me, I'd put it all into lengthy diatribes to my distant guru, Otto Frank."

That the designated guru replied, year after year, to embarrassing and shabby effusions like these may open a new pathway into our generally obscure understanding of the character of Otto Frank. His responses—from Basel, where he had settled with his second wife—were consistently attentive, formal, kindly. When Wilson gave birth, he sent her a musical toy, and he faithfully offered a personal word about her excitements as she supplied them: her baby sons, her dance lessons, her husband's work on commercials, her freelance writing. But his letters were also political and serious. It is good, he wrote in October, 1970, to take "an active part in trying to abolish injustices and all sorts of grievances, but we cannot follow your views regarding the Black Panthers." And in December, 1973, "As you can imagine, we were highly shocked about the unexpected attack of the Arabs on Israel on Yom Kippur and are now mourning with all those who lost members of their families." Presumably he knew something about losing a family. Wilson, insouciantly sliding past these faraway matters, was otherwise preoccupied, "finding our little guys sooo much fun.". . .

The young who are encouraged to embrace the diary cannot always be expected to feel the difference between the mimicry and the threat. And (like Cara Wilson) most do not. Natalie Portman, sixteen years old, who will debut as Anne Frank in the roadway revival this December of the famous play based on the diary—a play that has itself influenced the way the diary is read—concludes from her own reading that "it's funny, it's hopeful, and she's a happy person."

ANNE'S FATHER FOCUSES ONLY ON THE UPBEAT

Otto Frank, it turns out, is complicit in this shallowly upbeat view. Again and again, in every conceivable context, he had it as his aim to emphasize "Anne's idealism" "Anne's spirit," almost never calling attention to how and why that idealism and spirit were smothered, and unfailingly generalizing the sources of hatred. If the child is father of the man—if childhood shapes future sensibility—then Otto Frank, despite his sufferings in Auschwitz, may have had less in common with his own daughter than he was ready to recognize. As the diary gained publication in country after country, its renown accelerating year by year, he spoke not merely about but for its author—and who, after all, would have a greater right? The surviving father stood in for the dead child, believing that his words would honestly represent hers. He was scarcely entitled to such certainty: fatherhood does not confer surrogacy. . . .

TAKEN OUT OF CONTEXT

Perhaps not even a father is justified in thinking he can distill the "ideas" of this alert and sorrowing child, with scenes such as these inscribed in her psyche, and with the desolations of Auschwitz and Bergen-Belsen still ahead. His preference was to accentuate what he called Anne's "optimistic view on life." Yet the diary's most celebrated line (infamously celebrated, one might add)—"I still believe, in spite of everything, that people are truly good at heart"—has been torn out of its bed of thorns. Two sentences later (and three weeks before she was seized and shipped to Westerbork), the diarist sets down a vision of darkness:

> I see the world being slowly transformed into a wilderness, I hear the approaching thunder that, one day, will destroy us too, I feel the suffering of millions. . . . In the meantime, I must hold on to my ideals. Perhaps the day will come when I'll be able to realize them!

Because that day never came, both Miep Gies, the selflessly courageous woman who devoted herself to the sustenance of those in hiding, and Hannah Goslar, Anne's Jewish schoolmate and the last to hear her tremulous cries in Bergen-Belsen, objected to Otto Frank's emphasis on the diary's "truly good at heart" utterance. That single sentence has become, universally, Anne Frank's message, virtually her motto—whether or not such a credo could have survived the camps. Why should this sentence be taken as emblematic, and not, for example, another? "There's a destructive urge in people, the urge to rage, murder, and kill," Anne wrote on May 3, 1944, pondering the spread of guilt. These are words that do not soften, ameliorate, or give the lie to the pervasive horror of her time. Nor do they pull the wool over the eyes of history.

Otto Frank grew up with a social need to please his environment and not to offend it; that was the condition of entering the mainstream, a bargain German Jews negotiated
with themselves. It was more dignified, and safer, to praise
than to blame. Far better, then, in facing the larger postwar
world that the diary had opened to him, to speak of goodness
rather than destruction: so much of that larger world had
participated in the urge to rage. (The diary notes how Dutch
anti-Semitism, "to our great sorrow and dismay," was increasing even as the Jews were being hauled away.) After
the liberation of the camps, the heaps of emaciated corpses
were accusation enough. Postwar sensibility hastened to mi-
grate elsewhere, away from the cruel and the culpable. It
was a tone and a mood that affected the diary's reception; it
was a mood and a tone that, with cautious yet crucial exci-
sions, the diary itself could be made to support. And so the
diarist's dread came to be described as hope, her terror as
courage, her prayers of despair as inspiring. And since the
diary was now defined as a Holocaust document, the perception of the cataclysm itself was being subtly accommo-
dated to espressions like "man's inhumanity to man," dilut-
ing and befogging specific historical events and their
motives. "We must not flog the past," Frank insisted in 1969.
His concrete response to the past was the establishment, in
1957, of the Anne Frank Foundation and its offshoot the International Youth Center, situated in the Amsterdam house
where the diary was composed, to foster "as many contacts
as possible between young people of different nationalities,
races and religions"—a civilized and tenderhearted goal that
nevertheless washed away into do-gooder abstraction the
explicit urge to rage that had devoured his daughter.

THE DIARY NOW CONCEALS

Otto Frank was merely an accessory to the transformation of
the diary from one kind of witness to another kind: from the
painfully revealing to the partially concealing. If Anne Frank
has been made into what we nowadays call an "icon," it is
because of the Pulitzer Prize–winning play derived from the
diary—a play that rapidly achieved worldwide popularity,
and framed the legend even the newest generation has come
to believe in. Adapted by Albert Hackett and Frances Goodrich, a Hollywood husband-and-wife screenwriting team,
the theatricalized version opened on Broadway in 1955, ten

years after the end of the war, and its portrayal of the "funny, hopeful, happy" Anne continues to reverberate, not only in how the diary is construed but in how the Holocaust itself is understood. The play was a work born in controversy, destined to roil on and on in rancor and litigation. . . . Whatever the ramifications of these issues, whatever perspectives they illumine or defy, the central question stands fast: Who owns Anne Frank?

The hero, or irritant (depending on which side of the controversy one favors), in the genesis of the diary's dramatization was Meyer Levin, a Chicago-born novelist of the social-realist school, the author of such fairly successful works as *The Old Bunch, Complusion,* and *The Settlers.* Levin began as a man of the left, though a strong anti-Stalinist: he was drawn to proletarian fiction ("Citizens," about steelworkers), and had gone to Spain in the thirties to report on the Civil War. In 1945, as a war correspondent attached to the Fourth Armored Division, he was among the first Americans to enter Buchenwald, Dachau, and Bergen-Belsen. What he saw there was ungraspable and unendurable. "As I groped in the first weeks, beginning to apprehend the monstrous shape of the story I would have to tell," he wrote, "I knew already that I would never penetrate its heart of bile, for the magnitude of this horror seemed beyond human register." The truest telling, he affirmed, would have to rise up out of the mouth of a victim.

His "obsession," as he afterward called it—partly in mockery of the opposition his later views evoked—had its beginning in those repeated scenes of piled-up bodies as he investigated camp after camp. From then on, he could be said to carry the mark of Abel. He dedicated himself to helping the survivors get to Mandate Palestine, a goal that Britain had made illegal. In 1946, he reported from Tel Aviv on the uprising against British rule, and during the next two years he produced a pair of films on the struggles of the survivors to reach Palestine. In 1950, he published "In Search," an examination of the effects of the European cataclysm on his experience and sensibility as an American Jew. (Thomas Mann acclaimed the book as "a human document of high order, written by a witness of our fantastic epoch whose gaze remained both clear and steady.") Levin's intensifying focus on the Jewish condition in the twentieth century grew more and more heated, and when his wife, the novelist Tereska

Torres, handed him the French edition of the diary (it had previously appeared only in Dutch) he felt he had found what he had thirsted after: a voice crying up from the ground, an authentic witness to the German onslaught.

He acted instantly. He sent Otto Frank a copy of "In Search" and in effect offered his services as an unofficial agent to secure British and American publication, asserting his distance from any financial gain; his interest, he said, was purely "one of sympathy." He saw in the diary the possibility of "a very touching play or film," and asked Frank's permission to explore the idea. Frank at first avoided reading Levin's book, saturated as it was in passions and commitments so foreign to his own susceptibilities. He was not unfamiliar with Levin's preoccupations; he had seen and liked one of his films. He encouraged Levin to go ahead—though a dramatization, he observed, would perforce "be rather different from the real contents" of the diary. Hardly so, Levin protested: no compromise would be needed; all the diarist's thoughts could be preserved.

HOW THE DIARY WAS CHANGED

The "real contents" had already been altered by Frank himself, and understandably, given the propriety of his own background and of the times. The diary contained, here and there, intimate adolescent musings, talk of how contraceptives work, and explicit anatomical description. . . . All this Frank edited out. He also omitted passages recording his daughter's angry resistance to the nervous fussiness of her mother ("the most rotten person in the world"). Undoubtedly he better understood Edith Frank's protective tremors, and was unwilling to perpetuate a negative portrait. Beyond this, he deleted numerous expressions of religious faith, a direct reference to Yom Kippur, terrified reports of Germans seizing Jews in Amsterdam. It was prudence, prudishness, and perhaps his own deracinated temperament that stimulated many of these tamperings. In 1991, eleven years after Frank's death, a "definitive edition" of the diary restored everything he had expurgated. But the image of Anne Frank as merry innocent and steadfast idealist—an image the play vividly promoted—was by then ineradicable.

A subsequent bowdlerization, in 1950, was still more programmatic, and crossed over even more seriously into the area of Levin's concern for uncompromised faithfulness.

The German edition's translator, Anneliese Schütz, in order to mask or soft-pedal German culpability, went about methodically blurring every hostile reference to Germans and German. Anne's parodic list of house rules, for instance, included *"Use of language:* It is necessary to speak softly at all times. Only the language of civilized people may be spoken, thus no German." The German translation reads, *"Alle Kultur-sprachen . . . aber leise!"*—"all civilized languages . . . but softly!" "Heroism in the war or when confronting the Germans" is dissolved into "heroism in the war and in the struggle against oppression." ("A book intended after all for sale in Germany," Schütz explained, "cannot abuse the Germans.") The diarist's honest cry, in the midst of a vast persecution, that "there is no greater hostility than exists between Germans and Jews" became, in Schütz's version, "there is no greater hostility in the world than between these Germans and Jews!" Frank agreed to the latter change because, he said, it was what his daughter had really meant: she "by no means measured all Germans by the same yardstick. For, as she knew so well, even in those days we had many good friends among the Germans." But this guarded accommodationist view is Otto Frank's own; it is nowhere in the diary. Even more striking than Frank's readiness to accede to such misrepresentations is the fact that for forty-one years (until a more accurate translation appeared) no reader of the diary in German had ever known an intact text.

TRYING TO CREATE THE PLAY

In contemplating a dramatization and pledging no compromise, Levin told Frank he would do it "tenderly and with utmost fidelity." He was clear about what he meant by fidelity. In his eyes the diary was conscious testimony to Jewish faith and suffering; and it was this, and this nearly alone, that defined for him its psychological, historical, and metaphysical genuineness, and its significance for the world. With these convictions foremost, Levin went in search of a theatrical producer. . . .

Always delicately respectful of Frank's dignity and rights— and always mindful of the older man's earlier travail—Levin had promised that he would step aside if a more prominent playwright, someone "world famous," should appear. Stubbornly and confidently, he went on toiling over his own version. As a novelist, he was under suspicion of being unable to write drama. . . .

In the end—with the vigilant Levin still agitating loudly and publicly for the primacy of his work—Kermit Bloomgarden surfaced as a producer and Garson Kanin as director. [Lillian] Hellman [an important person in the theater world] had recommended Bloomgarden; she had also recommended Frances Goodrich and Albert Hackett. The Hacketts had a long record of Hollywood hits, from "Father of the Bride" to "It's a Wonderful Life," and they had successfully scripted a series of lighthearted musicals. Levin was appalled—had his sacred vision been pushed aside not for the awaited world-famous dramatist but for a pair of frivolous screen drudges, mere "hired hands"? . . .

FROM A JEWISH GIRL'S STORY TO A GENERIC PLAY

The Hacketts, too, in their earliest drafts, were devotedly "with the Jewish story." Grateful to Hellman for getting them the job, and crushed by Bloomgarden's acute dislike of their efforts so far, they flew to Martha's Vineyard weekend after weekend to receive advice from Hellman. "She was amazing," Goodrich crowed, happy to comply. Hellman's slant—and that of Bloomgarden and Kanin—was consistently in a direction opposed to Levin's. Where the diary touched on Anne's consciousness of Jewish fate or faith, they quietly erased the reference or change its emphasis. Whatever was specific they made generic. The sexual tenderness between Anne and the young Peter van Daan was moved to the forefront. Comedy overwhelmed darkness. Anne became an all-American girl, an echo of the perky character in "Junior Miss," a popular play of the previous decade. The Zionist aspirations of Margot, Anne's sister, disappeared. The one liturgical note, a Hanukkah ceremony, was absurdly defined in terms of local contemporary habits ("eight days of presents"); a jolly jingle replaced the traditional "Rock of Ages," with its sombre allusions to historic travail. (Kanin had insisted on something "spirited and gay," so as not to give "the wrong feeling entirely." "Hebrew," he argued, "would simply alienate the audience.")

Astonishingly, the Nazified notion of "race" leaped out in a line attributed to Hellman and nowhere present in the diary. "We're not the only people that've had to suffer," the Hacketts' Anne says. "There've always been people that've had to . . . sometimes one race . . . sometimes another." This pallid speech, yawning with vagueness, was conspicuously opposed to the pivotal reflection it was designed to betray:

> In the eyes of the world, we're doomed, but if after all this suf-fering, there are still Jews left, the Jewish people will be held up as an example. Who knows, maybe our religion will teach the world and all the people in it about goodness, and that's the reason, the only reason, we have to suffer. . . . God has never deserted our people. Through the ages Jews have had to suffer, but through the ages they've gone on living, and the centuries of suffering have only made them stronger.

For Kanin, this kind of rumination was "an embarrassing piece of special pleading. . . . The fact that in this play the symbols of persecution and oppression are Jews is inciden-tal, and Anne, in stating the argument so, reduces her mag-nificent stature." And so it went throughout. The particular-ized plight of Jews in hiding was vaporized into what Kanin called "the infinite." Reality—the diary's central condition—was "incidental." The passionately contemplative child, brooding on concrete evil, was made into an emblem of eva-sion. Her history had a habitation and a name; the infinite was nameless and nowhere. . . .

"I certainly have no wish to inflict depression on an audi-ence," Kanin had argued. "I don't consider that a legitimate theatrical end." (So much for "Hamlet" and "King Lear.")

THE CHEERFUL PLAY IS A HIT

Grateful for lightness, reviewers agreed. What they came away from was the charm of Susan Strasberg as a radiant Anne, and Joseph Schildkraut in the role of a wise and steadying Otto Frank, whom the actor engagingly resem-bled. "Anne is not going to her death; she is going to leave a dent on life, and let death take what's left," Walter Kerr, on a mystical note, wrote in the *Herald Tribune*. *Variety* seemed relieved that the play avoided "hating the Nazis, hating what they did to millions of innocent people," and instead came off as "glowing, moving, frequently humorous," with "just about everything one could wish for. It is not grim." The *Daily News* confirmed what Kanin had striven for: "Not in any important sense a Jewish play. . . . Anne Frank is a Lit-tle Orphan Annie brought into vibrant life." Audiences laughed and were charmed; but were also dazed and moved.

And audiences multiplied: the Hacketts' drama went all over the world—including Israel, where numbers of sur-

vivors were remaking their lives—and was everywhere successful. The play's reception in Germany was especially
noteworthy. In an impressive and thorough-going essay entitled "Popularization and Memory," Alvin Rosenfeld, a professor of English at Indiana University, recounts the development of the Anne Frank phenomenon in the country of
her birth. "The theater reviews of the time," Rosenfeld reports, "tell of audiences sitting in stunned silence at the play
and leaving the performance unable to speak or look one
another in the eye." These were self-conscious and thin-
skinned audiences; in the Germany of the fifties, theatregoers still belonged to the generation of the Nazi era. (On
Broadway, Kanin had unblinkingly engaged Gusti Huber, of
that same generation, to play Anne Frank's mother. As a
member of the Nazi Actors Guild until Germany's defeat,
Huber had early on disparaged "non-Aryan artists.") But the
strange muteness in theatres may have derived not so much
from guilt or shame as from an all-encompassing compassion; or call it self-pity. "We see in Anne Frank's fate," a
German drama critic offered, "our own fate—the tragedy of
human existence per se." Hannah Arendt, philosopher and
Hitler refugee, scorned such oceanic expressions, calling it
"cheap sentimentality at the expense of a great catastrophe."
And Bruno Bettelheim, a survivor of Dachau and Buchenwald, condemned the play's most touted line: "If all men are
good, there was never an Auschwitz." A decade after the fall
of Nazism, the spirited and sanitized young girl of the play
became a vehicle for German communal identification—
with the victim, not the persecutors—and, according to
Rosenfeld, a continuing "symbol of moral and intellectual
convenience." The Anne Frank whom thousands saw in
seven openings in seven cities "spoke affirmatively about
life and not accusingly about her torturers." No German in
uniform appeared onstage. "In a word," Rosenfeld concludes, "Anne Frank has become a ready-at-hand formula
for easy forgiveness."

ANNE HAS BECOME A CULTURAL PHENOMENON

The mood of consolation lingers on, as Otto Frank meant it
to—and not only in Germany, where, even after fifty years,
the issue is touchiest. Sanctified and absolving, shorn of darkness, Anne Frank remains in all countries a revered and comforting figure in the contemporary mind. In Japan, because

both diary and play mention first menstruation, "Anne Frank" has become a code word among teen-agers for getting one's period. In Argentina in the seventies, church publications began to link her with Roman Catholic martyrdom. "Commemoration," the French cultural critic Tzvetan Todorov explains, "is always the adaptation of memory to the needs of today."

But there is a note that drills deeper than commemoration: it goes to the idea of identification. To "identify with" is to become what one is not, to become what one is not is to usurp, to usurp is to own—and who, after all, in the half century since Miep Gies retrieved the scattered pages of the diary, really owns Anne Frank? Who can speak for her? Her father, who, after reading the diary and confessing that he "did not know" her, went on to tell us what he thought she meant? Meyer Levin, who claimed to be her authentic voice—so much so that he dared to equate the dismissal of his work, however ignobly motivated, with Holocaust annihilation? Hellman, Bloomgarden, Kanin, whose interpretations clung to a collective ideology of human interchangeability? (In discounting the significance of the Jewish element, Kanin had asserted that "people have suffered because of being English, French, German, Italian, Ethiopian, Mohammedan, Negro, and so on"—as if this were not all the more reason to comprehend and particularize each history.) And what of Cara Wilson and "the children of the world," who have reduced the persecution of a people to the trials of adolescence?

Who Owns Anne Frank?

All these appropriations, whether cheaply personal or densely ideological, whether seen as exalting or denigrating, have contributed to the conversion of Anne Frank into usable goods. There is no authorized version other than the diary itself, and even this has been brought into question by the Holocaust-denial industry—in part a spin off of the Anne Frank industry—which labels the diary a forgery. One charge is that Otto Frank wrote it himself, to make money. (Scurrilities like these necessitated the issuance, in 1986, of a Critical Edition by the Netherlands State Institute for War Documentation, including forensic evidence of handwriting and ink—a defensive hence sorrowful volume.)

No play can be judged wholly from what is on the page; a play has evocative powers beyond the words. Still, the Hackett's work, read today, is very much a conventionally well made Broadway product of the fifties, alternating comical beats with scenes of alarm, a love story with a theft, wisdom with buffoonery. The writing is skilled and mediocre, not unlike much of contemporary commercial theatre. Yet this is the play that electrified audiences everywhere, that became a reverential if robotlike film, and that—far more than the diary—invented the world's Anne Frank. Was it the play or was it the times? The upcoming revival of the Hacketts' dramatization—promising revisions incorporating passages Otto Frank deleted from the diary—will no doubt stimulate all the old quarrelsome issues yet again. But with the Second World War and the Holocaust receding, especially for the young, into distant fable—no different from tales, say, of Attila the Hun—the revival enters an environment psychologically altered from that of the 1955 production. At the same time, Holocaust scholarship—survivor memoirs, oral histories, wave after wave of fresh documentation and analysis—has increased prodigiously. At Harvard, for instance, under the rubric "reception studies," a young scholar named Alex Sagan, a relative of the late astronomer, is examining the ways Anne Frank has been transmuted into, among other cultural manifestations, a heavenly body. And Steven Spielberg's "Schindler's List," about a Nazi industrialist as savior, has left its mark.

How Should One Read the Diary?

It may be, though, that a new production, even now, and even with cautious additions, will be heard in the play's original voice. It was always a voice of good will; it meant, as we say, well—and, financially, it certainly did well. But it was Broadway's style of good will, and that, at least for Meyer Levin, had the scent of ill. For him, and signally for Bloomgarden and Kanin, the most sensitive point—the focus of trouble—lay in the ancient dispute between the particular and the universal. All that was a distraction from the heart of the matter: in a drama about hiding, evil was hidden. And if the play remains essentially as the Hacketts wrote it, the likelihood is that Anne Frank's real history will hardly prevail over what was experienced, forty years ago, as history transcended, ennobled, rarefied. The first hint is already in the air, puffed by the play's young lead: *It's funny, it's hopeful, and she's a happy person.*

Evisceration [removing the essential parts], an elegy for the murdered. Evisceration by blurb and stage, by shrewdness and naïveté, by cowardice and spirituality, by forgiveness and indifference, by success and money, by vanity and rage, by principle and passion, by surrogacy and affinity. Evisceration by fame, by shame, by blame. By uplift and transcendence. By usurpation.

On Friday, August 4, 1944, the day of the arrest, Miep Gies climbed the stairs to the hiding place and found it ransacked and wrecked. The beleaguered little band had been betrayed by an informer who was paid seven and a half guilders— about a dollar—for each person: sixty guilders for the lot. Miep Gies picked up what she recognized as Anne's papers and put them away, unread, in her desk drawer. There the diary lay untouched, until Otto Frank emerged alive from Auschwitz. "Had I read it," she said afterward, "I would have had to burn the diary because it would have been too dangerous for people about whom Anne had written." It was Miep Gies—the uncommon heroine of this story, a woman profoundly good, a failed savior—who succeeded in rescuing an irreplaceable masterwork. It may be shocking to think this (I am shocked as I think it), but one can imagine a still more salvational outcome: Anne Frank's diary burned, vanished, lost—saved from a world that made of it all things, some of them true, while floating lightly over the heavier truth of named and inhabited evil.

The Power of a Book

Roger Rosenblatt

Roger Rosenblatt is both a nonfiction author and an award-winning journalist. In this article for *Time* magazine's Top 100 People of the Century, he high-lights Anne Frank's inspiring ability to use her writing to rise above the horrible situation in which she lived. Her status as one of the "Top 100" people of the twentieth century is not only because she wrote a diary telling about her experiences in hiding, but also because "she is an extraordinarily good writer" with a "ruthlessly honest disposition." Despite the obvious social, historical, and cultural differences between a contemporary reader and Anne, Rosen-blatt writes that Anne has come to represent the hu-man experience of growing up and struggling to de-termine who and what one desires to be. Rosenblatt focuses on Anne's ability to put into words, in the midst of a nightmare, the thoughts and feelings that all human beings struggle with. Because of the con-nection she makes with her readers, the powerful optimism and sense of ultimate hope that she con-veys in her writing, and the sadness of her death, Anne has become one of the pivotal people repre-senting the twentieth century.

Along with everything else she came to represent, Anne Frank symbolized the power of a book. Because of the diary she kept between 1942 and 1944, in the secret upstairs an-nex of an Amsterdam warehouse where she and her family hid until the Nazis found them, she became the most mem-orable figure to emerge from World War II—besides Hitler, of course, who also proclaimed his life and his beliefs in a book. In a way, the Holocaust began with one book and ended with another. Yet it was Anne's that finally prevailed—a beneficent and complicated work outlasting a simple and evil one—and that secured to the world's embrace the second most famous child in history.

So stirring has been the effect of the solemn-eyed, cheerful, moody, funny, self-critical, other-critical teenager on those who have read her story that it became a test of ethics to ask a journalist, If you had proof the diary was a fraud, would you expose it? The point was that there are some stories the world so needs to believe that it would be profane to impair their influence. All the same, the Book of Anne has inspired a panoply of responses—plays, movies, documentaries, biographies, a critical edition of the diary—all in the service of understanding or imagining the girl or, in some cases, of putting her down.

"Who Owns Anne Frank?" asked novelist Cynthia Ozick, in an article that holds up the diary as a sacred text and condemns any tamperers. The passions the book ignites suggest that everyone owns Anne Frank, that she has risen above the Holocaust, Judaism, girlhood and even goodness and become a totemic figure of the modern world—the moral individual mind beset by the machinery of destruction, insisting on the right to live and question and hope for the future of human beings.

As particular as was the Nazi method of answering "the Jewish question," it also, if incidentally, presented a form of the archetypal modern predicament. When the Nazis invaded Holland, the Frank family, like all Jewish residents, became victims of a systematically constricting universe. First came laws that forbade Jews to enter into business contracts. Then books by Jews were burned. Then there were the so-called Aryan laws, affecting intermarriage. Then Jews were barred from parks, beaches, movies, libraries. By 1942 they had to wear yellow stars stitched to their outer garments. Then phone service was denied them, then bicycles. Trapped at last in their homes, they were "disappeared."

At which point Otto and Edith Frank, their two daughters Margot and Anne and the Van Pels family decided to disappear themselves, and for the two years until they were betrayed, to lead a life reduced to hidden rooms. But Anne had an instrument of freedom in an autograph book she had received for her 13th birthday. She wrote in an early entry, "I hope that you will be a great support and comfort to me." She had no idea how widely that support and comfort would extend, though her awareness of the power in her hands seemed to grow as time passed. One year before her death from ty-phus in the Bergen-Belsen camp, she wrote, "I want to be use-ful or give pleasure to people around me who yet don't really know me. I want to go on living even after my death!"

AN EXTRAORDINARILY GOOD WRITER

The reason for her immortality was basically literary. She was an extraordinarily good writer, for any age, and the quality of her work seemed a direct result of a ruthlessly honest disposition. Millions were moved by the purified ver-sion of her diary originally published by her father, but the recent critical, unexpurgated edition has moved millions more by disanointing her solely as an emblem of innocence. Anne's deep effect on readers comes from her being a nor-mal, if gifted, teenager. She was curious about sex, doubtful about religion, caustic about her parents, irritable especially to herself; she believed she had been fitted with two contra-dictory souls.

All of this has made her more "useful," in her terms, as a recognizable human being. She was not simply born blessed with generosity; she struggled toward it by way of self-doubt, impatience, rage, ennui—all things that test the value of a mind. Readers enjoy quoting the diary's sweetest line—"I still believe, in spite of everything, that people are still truly good at heart"—but the passage that follows is more reveal-ing: "I simply can't build up my hopes on a foundation con-sisting of confusion, misery and death. I see the world grad-ually being turned into a wilderness; I hear the ever approaching thunder, which will destroy us too; I can feel the sufferings of millions; and yet, if I look up into the heav-ens, I think that it will all come right, that this cruelty will end, and that peace and tranquillity will return again . . . I must uphold my ideals, for perhaps the time will come when I shall be able to carry them out."

Here is no childish optimism but rather a declaration of principles, a way of dealing practically with a world bent on destroying her. It is the cry of the Jew in the attic, but it is also the cry of the 20th century mind, of the refugee forced to wander in deserts of someone else's manufacture, of the invisible man who asserts his visibility. And the telling thing about her statement of "I am" is that it bears no traces of self-indulgence. In a late entry, she wondered, "Is it really good to follow almost entirely my own conscience?" In our time of holy self-expression, the idea that truth lies outside one's own troubles comes close to heresy, yet most people acknowledge its deep validity and admire the girl for it.

Indeed, they love her, which is to say they love the book. In her diary she showed the world not only how fine a person she was, but also how necessary it is to come to terms with one's own moral being, even—perhaps especially—when the context is horror. The diary suggests that the story of oneself is all that we have, and that it is worth a life to get it right.

It was interesting that the Franks' secret annex was concealed by a bookcase that swung away from an opening where steps led up to a hidden door. For a while, Anne was protected by books, and then the Nazis pushed them aside to get at a young girl. First you kill the books; then you kill the children. What they could not know is that she had already escaped.

The Definitive Edition of the Diary

Thomas Larson

Thomas Larson is an essayist whose focus in this article is on what the 1995 definitive edition of *The Diary of Anne Frank* teaches the reader about the true Anne Frank. With the publication of the 1995 edition, many original entries that had once been edited from the text were returned, and her diary was printed in its entirety. These additions shed new light on the complexity of Anne's character and her development as both a writer and as a young girl who is becoming a woman. The original, edited versions of her diary, as well as the original 1955 stage play, focused on an optimistic and girlish young Anne, leaving behind many of the hard questions and feelings that are found in the unabridged diary. The new edition does not change who Anne was, but allows the reader to see more of the negative aspects of her personality. Larson demonstrates that Anne had two sides, what he calls the "twin Annes." He argues that the reader of the new edition is able to love Anne as she really was, not simply because she was so optimistic and "good," but precisely because she is good and "bad," she is much more human.

The definitive edition of *The Diary of a Young Girl* by Anne Frank, published in English in 1995, restored her original entries which her father, the diary's compiler in 1947, had deleted from the first edition. Many of the new edition's reviewers (Or is it readers? Can one "review" Anne Frank's diary?) have expressed the standard adoring praise. In fact, one writer noted that even the reborn diary's 30 percent more material "does not alter our basic sense of Anne Frank." I didn't know we shared the same "basic sense" about her.

Thomas Larson, "In Spite of Everything: The Definitive Indefinite Anne Frank," *The Antioch Review*, vol. 58, Winter 2000, p. 40. Copyright © 2000 by Antioch Review, Inc. Reproduced by permission.

What is meant, I suspect, is that despite the additions Anne remains a victim par excellence, whose afterlife must forever gather together—and give thanks to—the penitent rememberers of the Holocaust. But studied carefully, away from Anne's iconolatry, the new edition disrupts this putative notion of her goodness. This version, in Susan Massotty's brilliant translation, is an even more incisive and tangled human document than the text that preceded it. True, Anne's anger with her parents and confusion with her own feelings were in the original diary. But now the definitive edition accumulates and intensifies so much more about her inner life that Anne's self-scrutiny dissuades us from enshrining her "goodness" and challenges us to love her honesty. (Which is what all teenagers seem to want!) This complete text discloses an author whose artistic subtlety and autobiographical truthtelling alone can command reverence. . . .

ANNE'S GLORY

The diary's privileged status is now fixed as the uniquely hopeful document against Nazi—and all—atrocities. And this portrayal has a long record of boosters. If we recall the expurgated diary's dissemination for junior high students beginning in the 1950s when Americans first read the book, or the robust optimism of the 1955 Pulitzer Prize–winning play by Albert Hackett and Frances Goodrich (screenwriters of *It's a Wonderful Life*), in which Anne's references to Jews as victims and Germans as killers were removed, or even the most "beautiful" Anne of all, Millie Perkins, and her maudlin forgiveness in George Stevens's 1959 film of the play, it is clear we've been bequeathed a child star of major proportions.

That was then—fifties' kitsch lacking the (current) politics of memory. Today, the wheel of Anne's glory rolls on, though the road is by no means smooth. Most notable is the documentary-rich but hagiographic-intended *Anne Frank Remembered*, whose director, Jon Blair, won the Oscar for Best Documentary film in 1996. While Blair's portrait achieved power with the stirring memories of Miep Gies, the courageous secretary who helped the Franks survive, and Janny Brandes Brilleslijper, who knew Anne at Bergen-Belsen where she died in 1945, some have criticized Blair for evangelizing Anne's precocity. One writer believed Blair had gone too far in "recreat[ing] and elevat[ing] Anne as some sort of commentator with absolute powers of perception" regarding the course of the war and the barbarity of the camps. In late 1997 a new version of the play opened on Broadway but to a ho-hum reception (it has since closed). The refurbishers folded in the new Anne, drawing out Jewish ethnicity, German culpability, and Anne's quarrels with her mother. But, even with more lines, Anne remained sapped of ego by the play's simplistic dialogue and saccharine emotion. The chief critic of Anne's marbled statuary is Cynthia Ozick whose 1997 *New Yorker* article "Who Owns Anne Frank?" castigated those who've exploited the diary in non-Jewish ways, sidestepping German evil as yet another anti-Semitic ploy.

FINDING ANNE TODAY

Anne's glorification continues at 263 Prinsengracht in Amsterdam, the site of the secret annex where she and seven others hid. Now a museum, it attracts over a half-million visitors a year. The Anne Frank Center USA promises to "educate the public, especially young people, about the causes, instruments, and dangers of discrimination and violence through the story of Anne Frank." AFCUSA gives out its "Spirit of Anne Frank Awards" each year and, with other groups, sponsors touring exhibitions that teach schoolchildren about the Jewish genocide through the more accessible video, photographic, and "hands-on" displays of life in the Franks' annex.

You can find Anne served up at several sites on the web, for example, the Virtual Anne Frank House. With a screen backdrop of torn sackcloth and ashes, and a "comprehensive" list of Anne Frank links, the Virtual House contains this opening gambit: "If you thoroughly explore this old business building . . . you may then be fortunate enough to stumble upon the hidden entrance to the secret Annex, where the True Anne is hiding; however, DO NOT expect it to be easy, as the portal has been hidden as well as the Franks hid theirs! Happy Hunting!" What an odd come-on, as naive as it is distasteful, which asks the site's visitors to adopt the role of Nazis searching for Jews in hiding! Lest we think this beyond the pale, consider that caricaturing the hunt for Jews at the Frank house may tell us just how untamishable the "True Anne" is.

The True Anne bears an intolerable burden: her visage— that clear smiling face amid the facelessness of mass killing—

must balance on its own the overtold horror of the Shoah [the Jewish word for the Holocaust]. How distant the diarist is from the icon! It is time to get away from the noble and poisonous appropriation her writing has suffered. It is time to understand how and why the author Anne Frank created, altered, edited, and then re-invented the character Anne Frank long before the euphemizers in theater and film had their say. Anne's "true" struggle with herself and how others should see her is evident only in the diary, in the written universe of her ego, that coarse contour of an embattled self which permeates the definitive edition.

So be warned: this new Anne is no longer one-dimensional. Her divided and divisive self presses out, especially in the longer entries of 1944 and the final three months of hiding, often with a vituperative tongue a bit like a pet snake. Now, returned to foil her popular cast, Anne is as contrarian as she was wise, enigmatic as she was forgiving. And though lowering her halo will be labeled "revisionist" (as if it were an unkind or dirty thing to do), Anne's diary, I think, can withstand any critical wringing. Her peevishness, her vitality, her conscience—cascading from an inspired pen, ages thirteen, fourteen, and fifteen when she wrote entries approximately twice a week during her two years in a cage— is inexhaustible, much like the endless problems we face with representing the Holocaust itself as messy truth instead of easy exaggeration.

THE DIARY REWRITTEN

The first edition of *The Diary of a Young Girl* appeared in Holland, in 1947. For that edition Anne's father, Otto Frank, carefully chose the least offensive parts of his daughter's diary, in which she wrote from her thirteenth birthday, June 12, 1942, to August 1, 1944. Otto Frank was the sole surviving member of the Frank family: Anne, her older sister, Margot, and their mother died in concentration camps as did the van Daan family, Petronella, Hermann, and young Peter (with whom Anne fell in love) and Albert Dussel, a dentist, the eighth person to hide with the Franks and the van Daans in the Secret Annex. At the time, Frank sanitized Anne's diary for several reasons. One, his Dutch publisher wanted the diary as part of a series of war remembrances, so cuts were necessary. Two, Otto Frank was wary of offending the memory of anyone in the Annex whom Anne had profiled unflatteringly, including himself. (Anne gripes often at her mother, the van Daans, and Mr. Dussel, less often at her father.) Third, Frank removed the more impudent and excessive self-indulgence that Anne at times revels in. He emphasized less her selfish desires as a young teenager and more her sacrifice to her family's needs. This is the book that was published in 1952, in its English edition, and universally cited as the most purchased, read, and admired secular book in history. As noted, millions of American teens, in the 1950s and 1960s, read the book in their English classes or else saw film or play versions of the diary. With good reason, the postwar generation wanted this noble, softer, innocent portrait to counter the horror—especially after the dispersal of newsreel footage of the concentration camps' liberation—of history's most concentrated genocide.

Otto Frank's 1947 diary (called diary c by Frank scholars) is a shorter version of two other documents that Anne actually wrote. Papa Frank produced his version from Anne's two diaries—an original unedited version (diary a) and her (not her father's) edited version (diary b), which she rewrote in 1944 and hoped to have published after the war. This diary b, which Anne developed by rewriting and fictionalizing her own earlier entries, began in early 1944 when she heard on a radio broadcast from the exiled Dutch government in London that a cabinet minister wanted to collect and publish "eyewitness accounts" of the war in the form of letters and diaries following Holland's liberation. According to the foreword of the definitive edition, an excited Anne "began rewriting and editing her diary, improving on the text, omitting passages she didn't think were interesting enough and adding others from memory."

RESTORED TO ITS ORIGINAL STATE

Using all three—Anne's unedited diary a, her edited diary b, and diary c which her father had printed in 1947—the 1995 definitive edition restores Anne's original work without its fictional elements and with all of its intense personal revelations. As noted, 30 percent is new, focusing on Anne's emerging sexuality, her passion for—and awkwardness with—Peter, and her snapping anger at her fault-finding mother as well as the histrionic Mrs. van Daan. The result is, the more her desires are shown (and the sexual ones are the least emphatic), the more her disarming honesty counters her self-sacrificing "goodness." The definitive diary reads as an act of discovery and of confusion, a journey that inevitably opens her "contradictions." By the end we are never sure if she's the author of or a character in the drama. But, despite her postmodern self, we feel her with all the hiss and bite and regret of a Thomas Hardy heroine.

Eventually the diary centers upon the intolerable proximity of confinement, but it begins as a flight, one might say a comfortable flight to safety. The Franks, the van Daans, and Mr. Dussel go into hiding with a large cache of money and, although the black market grows during their incarceration, they are able to buy most necessities. They have ample food because at least four people know where they are and regularly supply them. They have access to a toilet, a full kitchen, sleeping quarters (some with private rooms), a breeze and a view through uncurtained windows at night. They listen to the radio every night and have a small library. The three young people take correspondence courses and keep up with their studies as if they were in school. Each person's birthday is celebrated complete with gifts and a cake. Miep Gies, Otto Frank's secretary, does whatever she is asked, to keep the eight in essentials and occasional luxuries. On December 24, 1943, Anne writes, "I'm 'on top of the world' when I think how fortunate we are and compare myself to other Jewish children."

HER INNER WORLD CONSUMES ANNE'S THOUGHTS

I realize comfort should not lessen Anne's integrity. But she is given the time and space to write about herself in a cocoon around which a very distant war will rage. It is ironic that the Franks' confinement feels liberating enough for Anne to lay out her deepest fears and joys in her diary and, at the same time, the proximity of the Annex becomes Anne's main gripe, not the Nazis, not her fear of being discovered, not maintaining goodness in the face of impending evil. Because we get more of Anne's emotional analysis—especially the lengthier "negative" ones—the 1952 edition feels like a recollected romance of adolescence (how an adult would remember it) instead of a harsh account of a young girl's desperation in the 1995 edition.

What the added material underscores is how the outer world—the war, anti-Semitism, the internment camps, families being rounded up on the streets of Amsterdam, the nightly bombings, memories of her friends, the radio talk of invasion which arrives on June 6, 1944, two months before they are discovered—is subordinated in the first third of the diary to the claustrophobia of Anne's social life and is slowly turned inward by Anne, on Anne. She worries about starving children her age on the outside, yet complains about having to eat potatoes. She lectures herself about acting more responsibly around the adults, then fulminates at their intrusion on her privacy. She is curious about politics, which the adults usually argue at dinner, yet leaves off the discussion of war to lash out at her parents' favoritism of her sister. She knows the war hits the streets nightly, she fears betrayal and discovery, yet her venom stings and cuts at the adults in her midst whose neuroses have brought the war on in the first place. She is angry, at one time or another in the diary, at everyone, for they are complicit in ending the devil-may-care attitude of the young, her own in particular.

DID ANNE UNDERSTAND THE OUTSIDE WORLD?

Doesn't Anne know early on that what's happening outside is more important than her adolescent rumblings? Yes and no. Yes, because she is told about it often. When Mr. Dussel joins the Annex in late 1942, he brings news of the Jews' deportation to the camps: "The sick, the elderly, children, babies and pregnant women—all are marched to their death." Anne responds to Dussel's news with compassion. She feels that the Jews' misery on the outside is far greater than anything she has had to suffer. She feels guilty, "wicked [for] sleeping in a warm bed." She writes, "It's a disgrace to be so cheerful." After Mr. Dussel arrives, Miep Gies often tells the eight in the Annex of further deaths and deportations of friends. This makes the two mothers cry openly.

And no, because the increasing intensity from the war closing in on them makes Anne more conflicted in herself; as a consequence, she becomes more honest. Thus, Anne confesses something that, up to now, the first six months of confinement, she has been reluctant to admit. "Added to this misery there's another, but of a more personal nature, and it pales in comparison to the suffering I've just told you about. Still, I can't help telling you that lately I've begun to feel deserted. I'm surrounded by too great a void. I never used to give it much thought, since my mind was filled with my friends and having a good time. Now I think either about unhappy things or about myself. It's taken a while, but I've finally realized that Father, no matter how kind he may be, can't take the place of my former world. When it comes to my feelings, Mother and Margot ceased to count long ago."

FUNDAMENTALLY SELFISH

Fear liberates honesty. And Anne records her despair with such impact that its fundamental selfishness is easy to miss. She compares the "unhappy things" she thinks about to "myself," that is, makes self-sorrow equal to the bad that is happening outside. She feels abandoned by her family in the context of both personal and Jewish suffering. From this entry on, for eighteen months, Anne's isolation will torment and counsel her, for she is trapped between being protected and being abandoned by her family. Once that paradox becomes too much to bear, she will be trapped similarly by her surrogate parent, Peter.

For me, the great ignominy done to Anne Frank's diary arises from memory's oversimplifying those two "noble" sentences which she wrote near the end of their confinement, on July 15, 1944. "It's a wonder," she notes, "I haven't abandoned all my ideals, they seem so absurd and impractical. Yet I cling to them because I still believe, in spite of everything, that people are truly good at heart." For years, most diary readers have taken this admission unequivocally, a bald indication that goodness will triumph over evil. Why dispute it? Well, for one, it is not obvious at all who Anne is referring to by "people." Her parents? The Nazis? What are Anne's "absurd and impractical" ideals? And why does she insert that phrase—in spite of everything (what everything?)—as that which labors against those ideals?

ANNE'S IDEALS

Anne's "absurd and impractical" ideals are self- and family-related—being a good and loyal daughter, being a team player, thinking about the needs of others over her own. These are the ideals she cannot live up to (nor could anyone, under the circumstances). Anne's "everything" then is her experience alone, that is, the pressures of confinement that exacerbate the disapproval of those around her. Voiced by her mother and Mrs. van Daan, this disapproval of Anne's spontaneity is so excessive (i.e., truthful) that Otto Frank felt this was the easiest excision to make for that first edition.

But there are two problems with such editing. One, it gives a false balance between the outer and inner voices of her personality; and two, Anne's exaggeration contains much of the honesty that she may, in other passages, be trying to dress up or squelch. To excise the very honesty that Anne is most embarrassed by is to rob Anne of herself.

Consider this barrage: "Everyone thinks I'm showing off when I talk, ridiculous when I'm silent, insolent when I answer, cunning when I have a good idea, lazy when I'm tired, selfish when I eat one bit more than I should, stupid, cowardly, calculating, etc., etc. All day long I hear nothing but what an exasperating child I am, and although I laugh it off and pretend not to mind, I do mind. I wish I could ask God to give me another personality, one that doesn't antagonize everyone." In this and other invectives, the way Anne should act begins to grate on the Anne who, unseen, is acting as honestly as she can in her diary.

THE TWIN ANNES

The problem with "everything" referring to the "ideals" of a benevolent humanity is that, as Anne indicates many times, though she may believe in the goodness of others, she certainly does not believe it about herself. After eighteen months of diary writing, Anne re-reads her entire work, and she is "shocked" at the force of her "anger and hate" at her mother. "Anne, is that really you talking about hate?" she writes on January 2, 1944. "Oh, Anne, how could you?" This entry, six months before discovery, opens her up more than at any time to a writer's mystery of self, the reason her memoirist's pen is such a "friend." She discovers that there are (at least) twin "Annes" in the diary, Anne's bad self and Anne's reasonable being. She is apologetic, telling Kitty, her diary's other persona—as if taking it back will resolve it—that the Anne of the diary's first half was merely overcome by the pressures of hiding and whose disregard is extreme, false. "I was furious at Mother (and still am a lot of the time). It's true, she didn't understand me, but I didn't understand her either." Anne actually believes that it is her own "insolent and beastly" attitude toward her mother that caused her mother's unhappiness! And this: "Those violent outbursts on paper are simply expressions of anger that, in normal life, I could have worked off by locking myself in my room and stamping my foot a few times or calling Mother names behind her back." In other words, freedom and a normal adolescence would have produced an outlet for her anger to be directed—in the comfort of her own room—away from her mother. But in the Annex, the hiding from the world has produced a surfeit of honest responses in Anne for which she now feels shame. "I soothe my conscience," she ends the entry, "with the thought that it's better for unkind words to be down on paper than for Mother to have to carry them around in her heart."

Anne's self-psychologizing and her dislike of what she finds internally is perhaps her greatest revelation. Her guilt and shame that she has been too unforgiving with her mother are important. But what's crucial for knowing her totally are these emotional flip-flops. She is the sort of diarist who one minute writes, "Because she [her mother] loved me, she was tender and affectionate, but because of the difficult situation I put her in, and the sad circumstances in which she found herself, she was nervous and irritable" and, the next minute, "But there's one thing I can't do, and that's to love Mother with the devotion of a child." It's this agonizing complexity of a daughter's being that once it was born in the diary no doubt signaled Anne's father to deemphasize it. Cutting out that overintense self gives rise to Anne's "universality," her one-dimensionality. But I like the feisty liberator of self—the more Anne says she'll be more tolerant with Mom, the more such an admission only makes the stakes greater, the conflict sharper between who she is and what she "should be." Being the good Anne over the selfish Anne, perhaps her main ideal, is impossible to achieve. And, sure enough, the remainder of the diary belies her self-nobility, a fact she knows and reveals.

A ROMANCE IN HIDING

Peter, two years her senior, also meets the twin Annes. Anne seeks Peter out because he is easy to confide in; a few such meetings between them assures her that Peter can give Anne the uncritical support that her mother cannot and that her father seems to be increasingly withdrawing. Heightening Peter's accessibility are her dreamy memories of another Peter, a boy she knew during sixth grade whom she describes as "my one true love." She recalls how handsome he was, how much she pined for him when he moved away. She admits that the recollection of this boy has kindled her understanding of sexual desire.

Enter Peter van Daan who replicates in the Annex this other Peter—he too is handsome and soft and, best of all, present. Fantasizing about never seeing the old Peter again, she pursues the soft, kind, shy, unforward Peter in her midst. As the diary transforms the old Peter into the new one, so too does it separate the selfish, honest Anne from the diplomatic, considerate young girl. The split occurs in desiring Peter, and Anne delineates for the first time her internal break. "Suddenly," she writes, "the everyday Anne slipped away and the second Anne took her place. The second Anne, who's never overconfident or amusing, but wants only to love and be gentle." Anne sees, for now, her "true" self as the less honest being, the dutiful daughter to a mother she hates, the girl who must always be strong and never waver. For me, Anne's "true" self—which she will eventually recognize—is the teenager in love, breaking apart, repairing, breaking apart, truth-telling and fabricating.

The first Anne releases the second Anne and the latter falls for Peter, is enraptured by their sitting "in each other's arms" every night until Peter kisses her, awkwardly on the ear, which she prizes. But now, with Anne lost in love, the diary scuttles back and forth, sometimes within the same paragraph, between author and character, between the everyday Anne and the Anne who wants only to love. The character Anne writes, "Peter's reached a part of me that no one has ever reached before, except in my dream!" Which is followed by the author, thinking aloud about marriage. "What would my answer be? Anne, be honest! . . . Peter still has too little character, too little willpower. . . . He's still a child, emotionally no older than I am. . . . Am I really only fourteen? Am I really just a silly schoolgirl? . . . I'm afraid of myself, afraid my longing is making me yield too soon."

A Childish Anne Hurts Her Father's Feelings

When the adults see the pair getting too close, they first warn then forbid them to retire to the divan in the attic. Here Anne reaches her lowest point. Persisting every evening to "neck" with Peter upstairs, she writes her father a letter that tests his forbearance. The letter is a passionate claim for her independence; cooped up in the Annex for nearly two years, she's entitled to make her own decisions. She writes that, of course, "you [want me] to act the way a fourteen-year-old is supposed to. But that's where you're wrong!" She tells him "there's only one person I'm accountable to, and that's me." She says that she's been "putting on an act" for two years, having never revealed her true feelings: "I was overconfident to keep from having to listen to the voice inside me." To cap it off, Anne doesn't destroy the letter (as she later says she should have) but gives it to him!

His reply is a swift beheading of her independence. "I've received many letters in my lifetime," he says to her, in tears, "but none as hurtful as this. . . . No, Anne, you've done us a great injustice!" Her father's pain is her worst moment in the Annex: "What I'm most ashamed of is the way Father has forgiven me." To be independent of her parents when they have given her so much now becomes anathema for Anne, and it's all because her ideals over loving Peter got in the way of her duty.

Once Anne's dalliance with Peter and her attack on her father causes everyone pain, Anne discovers to her fear that she herself is more interesting and more split than anyone in the Annex. Even at fourteen, she realizes the import of her doppelganger nature. She wakes up to her paradoxical character largely because she has documented its growth. This conflict between author and character, first and second "Anne"s, is in the nature of diary-writing. The shadow-play of self-disclosure when recording experiences always inhibits and releases honesty. The indefiniteness occurs as the writer stumbles to get down what has happened and how she feels about it. We err to think Anne Frank's diary is merely "what happened" to her, mere events that contextualize the Holocaust. Her diary—any good diary—is primarily the deepest, most uncensored self-wringing through which any event or context comes to be recorded in the first place.

LEAVING ROMANCE BEHIND

The possibility of the diary, to reveal Anne completely to herself, now seems like an abyss for her, and she pulls back after the incident with her father. She drops Peter and the Anne who loved him. She hastens back to dutifully recording the family's struggles in the Annex. It is now May 1944, and the talk of the Allied invasion as well as noticeably fewer supplies take over the diary's content. In the lacunae, Anne's fear of fulfilling herself with Peter or with her own desires to be independent are swept under the surface of these practical entries. It's good, she seems to say, to be back in the comfort of family and worldly matters.

Another factor bringing her back is her decision, in April 1944, to make her diary publishable per the radio request of the Dutch cabinet minister. This means fictionalizing, editing, shaping—perhaps exaggerating?—what she has written so that the diary reveals more than just the record of their enclosure. In the last months Anne both keeps and rewrites her diary. Whether writing or editing, Anne senses that revealing her inner conflicts will make her document live and become published, preserved, known. Now it seems the first Anne, that "difficult" author-genie, will not go back in her bottle. And so the entries of the last three weeks in hiding grow more mature, complex, and daring. She can't get her "contradictions" onto paper fast enough once she sees that her inner life—not the latter-day purported cause of a degraded and ennobled humanity—is the diary's subject.

ANNE ANALYZES HERSELF

First Anne discovers that her own "self-reproaches" are where her wisdom lies. She now analyzes herself with the skill of a Viennese shrink. "What's so difficult about my personality is that I scold and curse myself much more than anyone else does." She hates it that others, her mother in particular, meet Anne's self-criticism with criticism, isolating Anne even more. "Then I talk back and start contradicting everyone until the old familiar Anne refrain inevitably crops up again: 'No one understands me.'" In one of her only post-romantic entries about Peter, she writes that his comfort used to help her with her trials of self but she admits that "he's disappointed me in many ways." He hides his "innermost self" from her and won't let her in. "He's much more closed than I am, but I know from experience . . . that in time, even the most uncommunicative types will long as much, or even more, for someone to confide in." With sudden maturity, Anne recognizes her personality conflicts as well as how they affect her and others. Seasoned diarist that she is, she is realizing that self-disclosure is her life.

Anne next trumpets the cause of women's liberation! She labels women who keep silent and go along with men's dominance, "stupid." "Fortunately, education, work and progress have opened women's eyes. . . . Modern women want the right to be completely independent!" She is also clear that women need not change into menlike beings—

stop having children, fight wars, etc. She sees the historical problem, male ignorance, as key. "What I condemn are our system of values and the men who don't acknowledge how great, difficult, but ultimately beautiful women's share in society is." What has occasioned these remarks is the book *Men Against Death*, which argued that women "suffer more pain, illness and misery than any war hero ever does." A reader senses with this entry in particular that the honest and complaining Anne, whom others and Anne herself have tried to censure, is now fearlessly saying what she believes.

Her final bloom, which for me solidifies what John Berryman called Anne's "conversion of a child into a person," at first seems to go her nascent self-analysis and feminism one better. She announces her "most outstanding character trait": "I have a great deal of self-knowledge. In everything I do, I can watch myself as if I were a stranger. I can stand across from the everyday Anne and, without being biased or making excuses, watch what she's doing, both the good and the bad. This self-awareness never leaves me." Anne is so sure of herself that she declares, "Ultimately, people shape their own characters." A remarkable statement this is, in the context of Nazi occupation! Indeed, in the Annex cage, how else but through self-examination and willfulness would Anne's character have been shaped and discovered?

LIVING WITH HER REGRETS

Anne's final power comes in realizing not her goodness but her regret. She regrets that her father "failed to see that this struggle to triumph over my difficulties was more important to me than anything else." She wanted what he couldn't give her: "To be treated . . . as Anne-in-her-own-right." She regrets that he has forced her to be someone she wasn't. "I've hid anything having to do with me from Father, never shared my ideals with him, deliberately alienated myself from him." Anne regrets having led Peter on, for doing so has been her "greatest disappointment." "I made one mistake," she writes. "I used intimacy to get closer to him, and in doing so, I ruled out other forms of friendship. . . . Our time together leaves him feeling satisfied, but just makes me want to start all over again."

With herself, finally, her regret sloughs through despair and confusion in the final diary entry. She blisters herself one last time by staying in her "contradictions," talking about how "I'm split in two." The one unpleasant Anne is the one she's known for, while the truer Anne "is my own secret," her "better side," which no one knows. As for her flippant side, the "exuberant cheerfulness," she writes, "You can't imagine how often I've tried to push away this Anne, which is only half of what is known as Anne—to beat her down, hide her." The reason, she says, is that others will ridicule her serious side, which is an incredible irony for it is this serious side that the diary exposes and for which she is beloved! And here, the great dilemma that all people face, aside from what their lives must represent, "I know exactly how I'd like to be, how I am . . . on the inside. But unfortunately I'm only like that with myself. And perhaps that's why—no, I'm sure that's the reason why—I think of myself as happy on the inside and other people think I'm happy on the outside. I'm guided by the pure Anne within."

WITHIN HER DIARY, ANNE FINDS HERSELF

The final two paragraphs of the diary end, perhaps arbitrarily, in this "who is Anne?" puzzlement. When things go bad or wrong, she ends up "turning my heart inside out, the bad part on the outside and the good part on the inside," even though she is "trying very hard to change myself, but that I'm always up against a more powerful enemy." That enemy is the public persona which for Anne is so misunderstood, which stands in the way of "what I'd like to be and what I could . . . if only there were no other people in the world."

Martyr to the Jews, so be it. But martyr to the unbridled adolescent self—this is undeniable. In fact, that last sentence contains a frightening admission—"no people" sounds genocidal, maybe suicidal. What has caused Anne the most pain is people, her coterie in the Annex who, she says, have never known her and have never, through their and Anne's fault alike, allowed the "pure Anne" out. People stifle us, the expectations of our parents, the unrequited love for another's hidden self that will not show itself. And yet, to be rid of people physically is not a literal idea. It is, instead, a metaphor for what the diary accomplishes: the removal of people so that her self, true and false and in-between, is allowed its freedom.

I don't think Anne ends in hatred of kin and romance; nor do I see her praising humankind, chattering on Churchill-like for decency and courage. I think the diary does what no film, play, traveling memorial exhibition, or preservation of the Anne Frank House in Amsterdam can ever accomplish—show us the intractable self, intractable from the beginning, all the way to the end, becoming even more intractable.

ANNE'S REAL VOICE IS SILENCED

Those final entries I have come to love—the rough, irreverent, stormy, disputatious Anne Frank, adulthood birthing itself in girlhood faster than girlhood can bear. The tragedy is that this voice, this emerging patchwork self—perhaps, had she lived, another witness of self-turmoil inside the Jewish nightmare, as honest as Elie Wiesel and Primo Levi—is silenced. Too suddenly the diary ends when the two families and Mr. Dussel are discovered and taken first to Westerhof to be sorted and transferred, and then shipped to concentration camps which, by the end of 1944, were actually shutting down, obliterating the evidence of the crematoria during the war's end-game. Anne with her older sister, Margot, dies of typhus in Bergen-Belsen in late February or early March 1945, six weeks before the camp is liberated by the Allies.

When Otto Frank read Anne's diary after the war, he said he was "surprised" by Anne's "self-criticism. It was quite a different girl than I had known as my daughter. She never showed these kind of inner feelings." This one statement, for me, almost wipes away the distortion of the first edition. His admission says that he understood the honesty and complexity of her writing; he didn't want the world to see and understand it as well. So we need not blame the father for missing his daughter's inner life. Rather, we are reminded of just how private we are, despite the openness of self-disclosure when others read our thoughts and feelings. It is a fact of the best diaries: they convince us that our hidden selves are our truest selves but, like Mr. Frank, we didn't notice it in the other, so busy were we hiding in our own privacy.

THE MANY FACES OF ANNE

To date, history has asked that we contextualize Anne Frank in her time—Jewish victim, recorder of one family's ultimately futile attempt to hide from the Nazis, precocious girl whose insights about prejudice and hatred we still learn from. And yet, it seems the more we contextualize Anne in her historical condition, the purer she becomes. Or, put differently, the result of the world's remembering her seems only to have purified her of herself.

No one can recast with new limbs and troubled heart the Holocaust's child; it may seem treasonous even to suggest it. But, by emphasizing this unknown, complicating, courageously individualizing person, who does emerge with arguably more horns than hopes in the definitive edition, we begin to acknowledge her multiplicity, begin to juggle and judge several "Annes": the pure and forgiving Anne of remembrance; the mother-conflicted feminist Anne; the writerly self-editing Anne; the self-reproachful and self-loathing Anne (easily the most unpopular one); the philosophical, contradictory, at times repressed, at times vindictive Anne; and Anne the Not So Innocent, who differs with us, I believe, about her further canonization, the Anne who is—perhaps—most like us.

Jewish Identity in Adaptations of the Diary

Jacob B. Michaelsen

Author Jacob B. Michaelsen is Professor Emeritus of
Economics at the University of California at Santa
Cruz. As a professor of economics, he studies Western religious and moral traditions and their effects
on the modern economy. Though his area of exper-
tise is economics, in this piece he outlines the path
that one twentieth-century author, Meyer Levin, took
in seeking to represent Anne Frank and the Holocaust in a meaningful way. Levin was an American
whose assistance was fundamental in getting Anne's
diary published in the United States. Michaelsen
documents Levin's desire to see an accurate and
probing look at Anne's life brought to the stage. Instead, Anne's father, Otto Frank, chose a non-Jewish
writing team to write and produce the play that
helped make Anne's life and death famous. In doing
so, Frank ensured that the play did not focus specifically on the Holocaust and the role that being Jewish
played in Anne's death. Levin, and others, have argued that in doing so, the play sanitized the awful
truth of World War II, and prevented the reader and
audience from asking the difficult questions that
must be asked if history is not to be repeated.

In 1995, fifty years after Anne Frank's death, the publication
of two books and the release of a documentary film shed
new light both on her life and on how the world has come to
know her. In *An Obsession with Anne Frank*, Lawrence
Graver, tells the story of Meyer Levin, an important, but neglected American writer, who was instrumental in bringing
the original version of Anne's Diary to the United States. Not

Jacob B. Michaelsen, "Remembering Anne Frank," *Judaism: A Quarterly Journal of
Jewish Life*, vol. 46, Spring 1997, p. 220. Copyright © 1997 by Jacob B. Michaelsen. Reproduced by permission.

long after its publication here, Levin had a quarrel with Anne's father, Otto Frank, over who would write the play based on the Diary. This conflict became an obsession for Levin that lasted the rest of his life. *The Diary of a Young Girl: The Definitive Edition* includes all the material Anne wrote, a significant portion of which Otto Frank removed in his initial editing. Otto Frank sought in the initial version to universalize the story as one of the consequences of intolerance in general, rather than of a virulent anti-Semitism in particular, and to portray Anne as tamer than the assertive and talented teenager that she was. It was this taming of Anne and of her story that led to the conflict between Levin and Otto Frank. And the Oscar-winning documentary, *Anne Frank Remembered*, provides a gripping portrait of Anne's life and of her death which, in its particularity, moves us away from Otto Frank's universalizing perspective and closer to Meyer Levin's understanding of what the Diary had to tell us.

An Obsession with the Story

The ground for Meyer Levin's obsession with Anne Frank was prepared during his service as a war correspondent in the European Theater during WW II. In that capacity, he accompanied American forces as they liberated the camps, including Bergen-Belsen, where Anne Frank died. Lawrence Graver tells us that "the camps touched the deepest sources of horror, anguish, and fear in his personality, and changed him for good. As he was later to say, 'Human beings had had it in them to do this, and we were of the same species.'" Levin committed himself to bear witness to this horror and, by implication, to discover how human beings could have conceived and carried out the Holocaust. Even as he sent dispatches back to America, he came to believe that writing this story was beyond his powers. "This tragic epic," he wrote, "cannot be written by a stranger to the experience. . . . Someday a teller would arise from amongst [the survivors]."

The story for which Levin waited did not come from a survivor. While living in France after the war, his wife, Teresa Torres, also a writer, came across the French version of *The Diary of a Young Girl* and brought it home. With the Diary, he had found a "teller." Levin threw himself into the project of bringing it to England and America and played a key role in getting it published in America in 1952. Levin saw early on that the Diary could be adapted for the theater and sought authorization to take on this project. Both Otto Frank, who edited the Diary, and Cheryl Crawford, its editor at Doubleday, agreed to give Levin a chance even though he had had no experience as a playwright. Levin agreed to work closely with a playwright if the draft he submitted was found to have sufficient promise. Graver tells us that Levin saw this as an opportunity to tell the story as he knew it and, as well, to establish his reputation as a major Jewish writer. . . .

LEVIN'S TEXT IS TOO JEWISH

Both Otto Frank and Cheryl Crawford, the Diary's editor at Doubleday, found Levin's draft of the play unacceptable. Rather than working further with him, they chose Frances Goodrich and Albert Hackett, co-authors of a number of successful plays, and it was their play that became a hit on Broadway and on which the 1959 movie was based. This decision, which gave this task to non-Jews who had not witnessed the horror directly, was the beginning of Levin's lifelong obsession with Anne Frank. Graver covers Levin's tortured path with great care and sympathetic understanding. We learn that Levin eventually brought suit against Otto Frank, made agreements with Frank and with the publisher that he failed to keep, advertised his complaints in newspapers and published a book about his obsession. Even though the market for work by Jewish writers writing on Jewish themes picked up after Word War II, he was unable to take advantage of it. Indeed, he saw the modest market for his early work to be the result of discrimination and the troubles he had with his version of the play as a continuation of it. Eventually one becomes frustrated with his pugnacity and paranoia and his inability to grasp that the world was not yet ready for the story he wanted to tell. . . .

To understand Levin's obsession, we need to get a firm grasp on what was at issue. Most importantly, Graver believes that Levin's play, which was produced only in Israel during Levin's lifetime and in Boston after Levin's death, is more authentic and much closer to the truth than the Goodrich-Hackett play, which reached multitudes the world over. "Working in a shoe-box-sized playing place, the Lyric Stage Company (of Boston) was able to communicate with great effectiveness the fright and claustrophobia of their inhabitants entombed in the hiding place, and much of the meaning of what happened to them there and afterward. That the two families and Dussel are Jewish is fundamental to the meaning. The Germans persecuted them for one reason, and this single fact shapes their response to their predicament."

ASKING THE WRONG QUESTIONS

We can get to the head of Levin's distress by examining a scene from the 1959 movie. Anne writes in the penultimate entry in her diary that "[i]t's a wonder I haven't abandoned all my ideals, they seem so absurd and impractical. Yet I cling to them because I still believe, in spite of everything, that people are truly good at heart." Near the end of the movie Anne dramatically proclaims this belief, not once but, twice. Few viewers will fail to get the message. Graver writes that "[m]ost theater-goers adored the Goodrich-Hackett Diary because they felt it transformed horror into something consolatory, inspirational, and even purgatorial: the characters may have been doomed, but the play was full of hope, energy, humor, lyricism, and 'ineradicable life.'" This famous exclamation about the character of the human heart occurs very near the end of Anne's text (July 15, 1944). In the remaining pages Graver notes, "Anne Frank followed . . . [it] with an apocalyptic vision of 'the ever approaching thunder,' destruction, and 'the suffering millions.'" For Levin, not only did this play not speak to how human beings could perpetrate the Holocaust; it did not even ask the question.

The response to the play in Germany where it was performed nearly 2,000 times and seen by more than a million people illustrates its problematic character. "Its sentimentality and evasiveness—its minimizing the Jewish subject in an effort to achieve an all-embracing, consoling universality—contributed to the tendency of many German playgoers to identify with the victims rather than see themselves as perpetrators." The Goodrich-Hackett play ends with knocking on the door. There are no SS troops, no camps, no open mass graves, no ovens. Graver believes that, ironically, the play may have accelerated the "long-delayed response to the Nazi past, especially among the young."

AVOIDING THE PAINFUL REALITY

It should not surprise us that, just after the war, the publisher did not want a play that confronted its audience with the "monstrous implications of the German attempt at genocide." Avoiding these implications was commonplace for years. The Eichmann trial in 1961 brought the matter forward in a dramatic way. And Israel, after the Six Day War in 1967, which many feared at the outset would become a second Holocaust, could now be seen as "acting as a very strong focus of worldwide Jewish emotional loyalty and thereby as a preservative of Jewish Identity." The success of the Israeli Defense Forces provided a much more secure basis than existed earlier for taking up these "monstrous implications." But in truth, it has taken decades for the horror to come out.

Levin misjudged what he was up against. In the beginning the issue was not personal; those who had a say in the matter believed that the public did not want what Levin had to offer. Nor did Otto Frank want it. Indeed, Otto Frank sought to make the Diary serve as a document of universal appeal against intolerance rather than one emphasizing the genocide of the Jews. In his editing "he omitted passages that fell generally into four categories: those that might offend living people, those that reflected negatively on his dead wife, those that were extremely intimate, and those he thought trivial and of little import." To illustrate the first category, the German edition prepared from the original Dutch-language diary, Anne notes the rule that everyone in the annex had to "speak softly at all times, in any civilized language, therefore not in German," becomes "all civilized languages but softly." Otto Frank made this change because of a desire not to offend some German friends.

OTTO FRANK STRIKES A HEALING NOTE

The Definitive Edition contains thirty per cent more material than the original version, much of it showing Anne as an assertive and talented teen-age girl rather than a flawless symbol. She criticized her mother extensively and often harshly. Her sister Margot, who was older, appears much more accepting. Still, Anne's criticisms seem within the bounds of normal complaint in mother-daughter relations for a person of Anne's temperament. Writing about them in her diary may well have helped her behave more decently toward her mother than she otherwise would have done. It is hard to believe that readers would see them as negative reflections on her mother. Anne writes of her discovery of her genitals and of her awareness of her growing sexuality.

This, too, gives the reader a chance to see Anne as a real person, giving vitality and power to her story. The omissions tell us as much about Otto Frank as about his daughter.

Graver provides an analysis of how Otto Frank came to have a view of the Diary and of the Holocaust so at variance with Levin's. . . .

As a person of modest and reserved temperament and one not given to verbalizing his "innermost thoughts and concerns" Otto Frank's need to rebuild his "shattered life" would lead him "to repress the horrors he had lived through." Feeling compelled to sound a healing note, "he felt confirmed in his constructivist instinct by daily letters from readers all over the world (the vast majority of them not Jewish) who testified that his daughter's rare book was an inspiring celebration of life in the face of hostile forces." But these readers had not, as Levin had, witnessed the liberation of the camps and seen the devastation, and they had not asked how human beings could have designed and built camps for the systematic destruction of an entire people.

A UNIVERSAL MESSAGE

The recent film, *Anne Frank Remembered*, which won an Oscar as a documentary in 1995, includes the story of Anne's last days in Bergen-Belsen. Hanneli Goslar, a school friend whose family had been taken, and about whom Anne had expressed concern in her diary, did survive. She told how, at Bergen-Belsen, she had thrown a package of clothing and food over a fence to her but never saw her again. Another survivor from Amsterdam, Janny Brandes, encountered Anne only days before her death, "stumbling, naked, in the freezing cold of that final winter at Bergen-Belsen. She had stripped off all lice-ridden clothes from her body and was barely wrapped in a gray blanket, sobbing, crying for help. She was all bone and tears and wide-eyed starvation, begging for clothes before she returned to the typhus-ridden body of her sister Margot, who lay near death."

Jon Blair, who directed the 1995 documentary, believed, along with Otto Frank, that the diary had a universalist message. Blair disagreed with those "who feel that the Holocaust was a uniquely Jewish experience and that Anne's story should be about the genocide of the Jews specifically." The film, however, belies Blair's stated intention: it does focus on the genocide of the Jews and, significantly, it does not include Anne's famous statement about the goodness of the human heart. Along with Levin, we must ask why the Jews were singled out for destruction, not for anything they had done, but simply for what they were. Because we now know Anne Frank in her particularity both in her life and in her death, we must struggle with Levin's question.

DISCUSSION QUESTIONS

CHAPTER 1

1. In the Melissa Müller article, Anne's earliest days are described. How did these early days help shape the young woman Anne was to become while in hiding?

2. Referring to the article by Isabel Reynolds, describe Anne's personality and what kind of friend she was.

3. Rachel Feldhay Brenner argues in her book that Anne took part in "resistance" to the war. Since Anne spent the greater part of the war in hiding, can Brenner's statement be true? Citing the text, discuss the ways in which Anne might have resisted the Germans in the war.

4. Denise de Costa writes of Anne's differences from mainstream society. Name three ways that Anne acted which placed her in the role of "the other."

5. Many young people were forced to go into hiding during the war. Though Anne is the most famous, she is hardly typical. Using the selection by Jacob Boas, compare Anne's experience to those of other young Jews in that time.

CHAPTER 2

1. Though the members of the annex knew that being arrested was a risk, the day it finally happened caught them off guard. In Ernst Schnabel's article about their arrest, he shares what happened in their final moments in the annex. How does this knowledge change what Anne herself wrote just days before the arrest? (See Appendix, Document 11.)

2. In Chapter 1, the article by Isabel Reynolds shares the memories of one of Anne's friends. Alison Leslie Gold writes about the memories of another childhood friend, Hannah Goslar. How do these two pictures of Anne compare? Cite similarities and differences.

3. The final two articles of this chapter contain memories of

Anne's final moments in camp. Though neither of the ladies interviewed had known Anne before the camps, each has distinct memories of her. What about Anne caused her to stand out? In what ways do the memories of these interviewees give us a fuller picture of Anne's final days in Bergen-Belsen?

CHAPTER 3

1. After the successful publication of Anne's diary, some people remained unconvinced that it was really written by a young girl in hiding. Gerrold van der Stroom writes about the intensive process that was used to prove the diary to be genuine. Why would someone doubt its authenticity? How do the proofs van der Stroom writes of convince a reader that it is real?

2. Because of her death Anne never had the opportunity to become a journalist and writer as she had dreamed. Anne Frank expert Mirjam Pressler asserts that, based on Anne's writings alone, Anne would have been a successful writer. Cite three examples of why this could be an accurate assumption.

3. Though Anne wrote an intimate and personal diary, author Hedda Rosner Kopf argues that the diary can also be read as a piece of literature. What characteristics of Anne's writing makes this possible?

CHAPTER 4

1. In her controversial article, Cynthia Ozick questions whether the diary would have been better off unpublished. What are her arguments for this? Are there any arguments that would prove Ozick wrong?

2. Thomas Larson writes that the new edition of Anne Frank's diary reveals a deeper and more complex Anne. Does this deeper knowledge of Anne encourage or discourage the reader to connect with Anne as a person?

3. Several articles in this chapter focus on the question of how Anne's diary should be read, arguing that she should not be considered representative of Jews during the Holocaust. Is this a convincing argument? How did Anne's experience differ from other Jews' during this time?

Appendix of Documents

Document 1: An Essay on Asking "Why?"

Though Anne Frank is known for her famous diary, she was also the writer of many essays and short stories. This selection, focusing on the importance of asking "why?" is one of her more serious essays and gives the reader a deeper sense of her probing personality.

The little word "why" has been a very strong thing with me ever since I was a tiny little girl and couldn't even speak properly. It is a well-known fact that little children ask questions about everything because they are unfamiliar with everything. This was very much the case with me, but even when I grew older I couldn't wait to ask all kinds of questions, whether they could be answered or not. This is not so terrible in itself and I must say that my parents tried to answer every one of my questions very patiently, until . . . I began even badgering strangers, and *they* generally can't stand "children's endless questions." I must admit that this can be very tiresome, but I console myself with the idea that there is a saying that "you must ask in order to know," which couldn't be completely true, otherwise I'd be a professor by now.

When I grew older, I realized that it is not possible to ask every kind of question to everyone and that there are many "why's" that cannot be answered. It then followed from that that I tried to help myself by starting to think out these questions on my own. So I came to the important discovery that questions which one mustn't ask can be solved by oneself. Therefore, the little word "why" taught me not only to ask but to think.

Now as to the second part of the word "why." How would it be if everyone who did anything asked himself first, "Why?" I think they would then become more honest and much, much better people. For the best way to become honest and good is to keep examining oneself without stopping. I can imagine that the last thing people like to do is to confess to themselves their faults and their bad side (which everybody has). This is the case with children as well as grownups—in that respect I don't see any difference. Most people think parents should try to educate their children and see to it themselves that their characters develop as well as possible. This is certainly untrue. Children ought to educate themselves from their earliest youth and must try to show real character by themselves.

Many will think this is crazy, but it isn't. Even a very small child is a little personality and has a conscience and should be brought up by being treated this way, so that it will feel that its own conscience is punishing it in the harshest way possible. When children reach the age of fourteen or fifteen, every punishment is ridiculous. Such a child knows very well that no one, not even his own parents, can get anywhere with punishments and spankings. By arguing reasonably and by showing the child the mistakes it is making, one would get much better results than by strong punishments.

But here, I don't want to sound pedantic, but only to say that in the life of every child and every man, the little word "why" plays a big part, and rightly so. The saying, "You must ask in order to know," is true in so far as it leads to thinking about things, and by thinking nobody can ever get worse but will only get better.

Anne Frank, *Anne Frank's Tales from the Secret Annex*, trans. Ralph Manheim and Michel Mok. New York: Bantam Books, 1994.

DOCUMENT 2: ANNE AS THE SERIOUS WRITER

The following is taken from Miep Gies's memoir of her time helping to hide the Frank family. She shares here the seriousness with which Anne took her writing.

I saw that Anne was writing intently, and hadn't heard me. I was quite close to her and was about to turn and go when she looked up, surprised, and saw me standing there. In our many encounters over the years, I'd seen Anne, like a chameleon, go from mood to mood, but always with friendliness. She'd never been anything but effusive, admiring, and adoring with me. But I saw a look on her face at this moment that I'd never seen before. It was a look of dark concentration, as if she had a throbbing headache. This look pierced me, and I was speechless. She was suddenly another person there writing at the table. I couldn't say a word. My eyes were locked with Anne's brooding ones.

Mrs. Frank must have heard me come in, and I heard her soft step beside me. I could tell from the sound of her voice when she finally spoke that she'd summed up the situation. She spoke in German, which she used only when a situation was difficult. Her voice was ironic, and yet kind. "Yes, Miep, as you know, we have a daughter who writes."

At this, Anne stood up. She shut the book she was writing in and, with that look still on her face, she said, in a dark voice that I'd also never heard before, "Yes, and I write about you, too."

She continued to look at me, and I thought, I must say something; but all I could say, in as dry a tone as I could muster, was "That will be very nice."

I turned and went away. I was upset by Anne's dark mood. I knew that more and more her diary had become her life. It was as if I had interrupted an intimate moment in a very, very private friendship. I went back downstairs to the office, feeling distressed and thinking all the rest of the day, It wasn't Anne up there. She was so upset by my interruption, it was another person.

Miep Gies and Alison Leslie Gold, *Anne Frank Remembered: The Story of the Woman Who Helped to Hide the Frank Family.* New York: Simon & Schuster, 1987.

DOCUMENT 3: ANNE DECLARES HER DESIRE TO BE PUBLISHED

Anne continues to work toward becoming a "real" writer. In this very brief selection from May 1944, just three months before she is arrested, she states her deep desire to publish her diary.

Kitty, can you see that I'm just about bursting?

Now, about something else: you've known for a long time that my greatest wish is to become a journalist someday and later on a famous writer. Whether these leanings towards greatness (or insanity?) will ever materialize remains to be seen, but I certainly have the subjects in my mind. In any case, I want to publish a book entitled *Het Achterhuis* after the war. Whether I shall succeed or not, I cannot say, but my diary will be a great help. I have other ideas as well, besides *Het Achterhuis*. But I will write more fully about them some other time, when they have taken a clearer form in my mind.

Yours, Anne

Anne Frank, *Anne Frank: The Diary of a Young Girl*, trans. B.M. Mooyaart-Doubleday. New York: Pocket Books, 1972.

DOCUMENT 4: THE MOST FAMOUS STATEMENT

Just a few short weeks before her arrest, Anne writes what is undoubtedly her most famous statement: "In spite of everything, I still believe that people are really good at heart." Though this quote is full of hope and often inspires many, it is made within the context of despair and uncertainty.

"For in its innermost depths youth is lonelier than old age." I read this saying in some book and I've always remembered it, and found it to be true. Is it true then that grownups have a more difficult time here than we do? No. I know it isn't. Older people have formed their opinions about everything, and don't waver before they act. It's twice as hard for us young ones to hold our ground, and maintain our opinions, in a time when all ideals are being shattered and destroyed, when people are showing their worst side, and do not know whether to believe in truth and right and God.

Anyone who claims that the older ones have a more difficult time here certainly doesn't realize to what extent our problems weigh down on us, problems for which we are probably much too young, but which thrust themselves upon us continually, until, after a long time, we think we've found a solution, but the solution doesn't seem able to resist the facts which reduce it to nothing again. That's the difficulty in these times: ideals, dreams, and cherished hopes rise within us, only to meet the horrible truth and be shattered.

It's really a wonder that I haven't dropped all my ideals, because they seem so absurd and impossible to carry out. Yet I keep them, because in spite of everything I still believe that people are really good at heart. I simply can't build up my hopes on a foundation consisting of confusion, misery, and death. I see the world gradually being turned into a wilderness, I hear the ever approaching thunder, which will destroy us too, I can feel the sufferings of millions and yet, if I look up into the heavens, I think that it will all come right, that this cruelty too will end, and that peace and tranquillity will return again.

In the meantime, I must uphold my ideals, for perhaps the time will come when I shall be able to carry them out.

Yours, Anne

Anne Frank, *Anne Frank: The Diary of a Young Girl*, trans. B.M. Mooyaart-Doubleday. New York: Pocket Books, 1972.

DOCUMENT 5: HOW ANNE'S DIARY WAS SAVED

In her memoir, protector Miep Gies recalls the day following the arrest of Anne and the other residents of the annex. Going back into the annex with her co-worker, she finds and gathers all of Anne's personal writings, safely storing them until Anne's father returns.

We opened the door and went into the hiding place.

Right away, from the door, I saw that the place had been ransacked. Drawers were open, things strewn all over the floor. Everywhere objects were overturned. My eyes took in a scene of terrible pillage.

Then I walked into Mr. and Mrs. Frank's bedroom. On the floor, amidst the chaos of papers and books, my eye lit on the little red-orange checkered, cloth-bound diary that Anne had received from her father on her thirteenth birthday. I pointed it out to Elli. Obeying my gesture, she leaned down and picked it up for me, putting it into my hands. I remembered how happy Anne had been to receive this little book to write her private thoughts in. I knew how precious her diary was to Anne. My eyes scanned the rubble for more of Anne's writings, and I saw the old accounting books and many more writing papers that Elli and I had given to her when she had run out of pages in the checkered diary. Elli was still very scared, and looked to me for direction. I told Elli, "Help me pick up all Anne's writings."

Quickly, we gathered up handfuls of pages in Anne's scrawling handwriting. My heart beat in fear that the Austrian would return and catch us among the now-captured "Jewish possessions." . . .

Trying not to drop anything, I bent to lock the door to the hiding place and returned to the office.

There Elli and I stood facing each other, both loaded down with papers. Elli said to me, "You're older; you must decide what to do."

I opened the bottom drawer of my desk and began to pile in the diary, the old accounting books, and the papers. "Yes," I told Elli, "I will keep everything." I took the papers she was holding and continued filling the drawer. "I'll keep everything safe for Anne until she comes back."

I shut the desk drawer, but I did not lock it.

Miep Gies and Alison Leslie Gold, *Anne Frank Remembered: The Story of the Woman Who Helped to Hide the Frank Family.* New York: Simon & Schuster, 1987.

DOCUMENT 6: THE EFFECTS OF READING THE DIARY

The Diary of Anne Frank had been through two printings before Miep Gies had the courage to read it. Here, she writes about her first reading, and the effect that it had on her, so long after losing her young friend.

The next time I was totally alone, on a warm day, I took the second printing of the diary, went to my room, and shut the door.

With awful fear in my heart, I opened the book and turned to the first page.

And so I began to read.

I read the whole diary without stopping. From the first word, I heard Anne's voice come back to speak to me from where she had gone. I lost track of time. Anne's voice tumbled out of the book, so full of life, moods, curiosity, feelings. She was no longer gone and destroyed. She was alive again in my mind.

I read to the very end. I was surprised by how much had happened in hiding that I'd known nothing about. Immediately, I was thankful that I hadn't read the diary after the arrest, during the final nine months of the occupation, while it had stayed in my desk drawer right beside me every day. Had I read it, I would have had to burn the diary because it would have been too dangerous for people about whom Anne had written.

When I had read the last word, I didn't feel the pain I'd anticipated. I was glad I'd read it at last. The emptiness in my heart was eased. So much had been lost, but now Anne's voice would never be lost. My young friend had left a remarkable legacy to the world.

But always, every day of my life, I've wished that things had been different. That even had Anne's diary been lost to the world, Anne and the others might somehow have been saved.

Not a day goes by that I do not grieve for them.

Miep Gies and Alison Leslie Gold, *Anne Frank Remembered: The Story of the Woman Who Helped to Hide the Frank Family.* New York: Simon & Schuster, 1987.

DOCUMENT 7: GOING INTO HIDING

While many Jews were forced into hiding like Anne and her family, not all were as fortunate to be in the healthy and relatively spacious quarters that Anne was. Renee G. writes of hiding with her family of eight in a hole dug into the ground.

My dad came and told me not to worry, that he found a place in a stable underground, a pit about five-by-eight, dug underneath the stable underneath the manure. I thought it was just the greatest thing to be together. Boards [were] propping up the ceiling and some of the side walls. There were two long benches on the side and one bench in the middle. The bench in the middle served as a table in the daytime. At night, that middle bench was leveled with the other two benches so we were able to sleep sideways, eight of us. We stayed there for about—well, for them it was almost two years. For me it was about fifteen months. The food consisted of morning coffee made from burned grain and a loaf of bread for eight people every other day. Lunch consisted of soup and occasionally some potatoes in it. Supper was again coffee. They used burned wheat to make the coffee. If we wanted to take a bath or wash our hair, we had to use our share of coffee.

We only could go out one at a time, because in case of danger we had to get in very quickly and close the opening. We were sealed in, almost without air. A couple of times people were passing out. This farmer was a very poor farmer, and when the idea came about of possibly hiding out eight Jews, this good farmer [the one who had previously helped them] negotiated with him for money, that we would pay him so much a month. The manure was laid on top, so that it was the same level as the whole stable. The ground with the animals [was] right over us, so nobody could tell there was anything going on underneath. And the farmer usually brought in food for the animals anyway, so the neighbors thought that the food was for animals.

The two female cousins bribed my [cousin] Oscar, the one who kept the diary of the war in hiding to teaching us language and math. He bargained for paper. He said, "If you can get me paper, I will give you lessons in those things." He himself and his father were going crazy for lack of activities. [He] one night risked his life and went to one of the ghettos that was still existing. It was a good forty kilometers away, and [he] went to go to that town to get books and came back with a sack full of books. So naturally, we read these books over and over and over again. I learned plain arithmetic, I believe, and perhaps we got into algebra. He taught us the Polish language and a little bit of English. . . . The books we read were mostly in Yiddish.

The biggest treat was when a newspaper came in. Every time that the farmer went to market, we put in our order. We would give him something extra to bring the paper for us. We would follow the war, and I remember the big heading of Stalingrad. And also we had to feed him information to encourage him that there was an end to all this, because several times he came in and he said, "No

more! You are getting out tonight! I'm chasing you out! I'm not risk-
ing my life anymore." Besides, we ran out of money. I think the last
three months or so, we didn't have any more money to give him
and he wanted to chase us out. We kept on encouraging him that
there will be money after we get out and we'll pay him back, and
that [the] war was almost over. We would show him the headlines
in German, which he couldn't read anyway. Finally one day, he was
in a good mood—I think maybe some good news came through or
some other farmer told him that the Russians were coming close.
He came in and he said, "Well, maybe we're actually making it after all." He says, "I'm not chasing you out anymore." He said, "I now
like you." He says, "You are almost as good as my cow and my
sheep and my pigs. I've gotten used to you," he said.

When my birthday came around, my dad wanted me to have
something special for dinner. He asked me what I want and I said,
"I would love to have some scrambled eggs." So he traded. He gave
the farmer a pair of golden earrings to get me scrambled eggs. And
I'll never forget, those were the best-tasting scrambled eggs I have
ever had in my life.

Joshua M. Greene and Shiva Kumar, eds., *Witness: Voices from the Holocaust*. New
York: The Free Press, 2000.

DOCUMENT 8: AN AIR-RAID IN HOLLAND

*Dirk Van der Heide was a twelve-year-old boy living in Holland. This
excerpt is from his diary, which he wrote during the war. Although
he was not in hiding like Anne Frank, he did experience the effects
of war, as evidenced by his remembrance of this Nazi air raid which
devastated the street on which he lived.*

Saturday, May 11, 1940: The worst air-raid of all has just come.
About half the houses on our street are gone. One bomb landed on
the lawn by our air-shelter and one side of the shelter is caved in
but the Baron and others are repairing it now. Mevrouw Hartog
broke down and cried during the air-raid and got everyone very
nervous when she yelled. I think she almost went crazy.

Heintje Klaes was killed! He went outside to see the light from the
big flares and incendiary bombs and didn't come back. He slipped
out. Heintje was not afraid of anything but the bombs got him. The
whole house rocked when the bombs came close. We put our fingers
in our ears but it didn't help much. The fire wagons are working outside now and half the people in the air-shelter including Uncle Pieter
have gone out. I went out for a while and they were taking dead
people out of the bombed houses. Uncle Pieter sent me back to stay
with Keetje. There is a funny smell in the air like burnt meat and a
funny yellow light all over the country from the incendiary bombs.
Three men were killed trying to get a bomb away that hadn't gone off
yet. One of the men was our postmaster and I loved him very much.
He gave me my first bicycle ride. It is awful to watch the people

standing by their bombed houses. They don't do much. They just walk around and look at them and look sad and tired. I guess there isn't anything else they can do, but it seems awful.

Our house wasn't hit but the street in front of it between our house and the Baron's is just a great big hole and all the cobble-stones are thrown up on our lawn and the Baron's until it doesn't look as if there ever was a street there. Mother is going to be sur-prised when she sees it. The street was just made over last year and was very smooth and nice.

At the end of our street the water is coming in where the canal locks were hit and I guess it will just keep running over the land until it is fixed. No one does anything about it because there are too many people to be helped and fires to fight. Twelve people on our street were killed and I knew every one of them but I knew Heintje best. Mevrouw Klaes has been crying ever since the bombing. Some people prayed all the time and some sang the national an-them and some just sat and stared. A woman who is very sick with a bad heart looked as if she might die. She was very pale when she came and still is.

I said a prayer to myself for Father and I hope God heard it in spite of all the noise. I told Uncle Pieter I had prayed but he didn't say anything, just laid his hand on my shoulder. Uncle Pieter has gone off to the hospital to try to find Mother. It is getting late and he is worried I think. I know he will find her. Keetje has gone to sleep again but she talks in her sleep and wakes up all the time, asking if the war is over and things like that. Poor Keetje, she is so little and doesn't know what is happening. I think I do and it is worse than anything I ever heard about and worse than the worst fight in the cinema. The ambulances coming and going and so many dead people make it hard for me not to cry. I did cry some while the bombing was going on but so many other little children were that no one noticed me I think. I just got into bed with Keetje and hid my face. I was really frightened this time.

Laurel Holliday, ed., *Children in the Holocaust and World War II: Their Secret Diaries.* New York: Washington Square Press, 1995.

DOCUMENT 9: LIFE AT WESTERBORK

Etty Hillesum was a Dutch Jew. Like Anne, she and her family were arrested and sent to Westerbork transit camp. She was ultimately moved to Auschwitz, where she died at the age of 29. This is from a letter she wrote describing life at Westerbork.

Not much heath is left now inside the barbed wire; more barracks are always being added. Only a little piece remains in the furthest corner of the camp, and that's where I'm sitting now, in the sun un-der a glorious blue sky, among some low shrubbery. Right across from me only a few meters away, a blue uniform with a helmet stands in the watchtower. A guard with an enraptured expression is picking purple lupins, his gun dangling on his back. When I look to the left I see billowing white smoke and hear the puffing of a loco-motive. The people have already been loaded onto the freight cars; the doors are closed. There are many green police, who sang this morning as they marched by the side of the train, and the Dutch military police are out as well. The quota of people who must go is not yet filled. Just now I met the matron of the orphanage, carrying a small child in her arms who also has to go, alone. And a number of people have been taken out of the hospital barracks. They are do-ing a thorough job here today; big shots from the Hague have come on a visit. It's very strange watching these gentlemen at work from close quarters. I've been up since four this morning dealing with the babies and carrying luggage. In a few hours you can accumulate enough gloom here to last a lifetime. The nature-loving policeman has gathered his purple bouquet now, perhaps he's off to court some farmer's daughter in the neighborhood. The engine gives a piercing shriek. The whole camp holds its breath; another three thousand Jews are about to leave. There are babies with pneumonia lying in the freight cars. Sometimes what goes on here seems totally unreal. I haven't been given any particular job, which suits me very well. I just wander about and find my own work. This morning I had a brief talk with a woman who had come from Vught, who told me her latest experiences in three minutes. How much can you really tell in a few minutes? When we came to a door, and I wasn't allowed to go any further, she embraced me and said: "Thank you for being such a help."

Just now I climbed up on a box lying among the bushes here to count the freight cars. There were thirty-five, with some second-class cars at the front for the escorts. The freight cars had been completely sealed, but a plank had been left out here and there, and people put their hands through the gaps and waved as if they were drowning.

The sky is full of birds, the purple lupins stand up so regally and peacefully, two little old women have sat down on the box for a chat, the sun is shining on my face—and right before our eyes, mass murder. The whole thing is simply beyond comprehension.

Etty Hillesum, *Letters from Westerbork*, trans. Arnold J. Pomerans. New York: Pantheon Books, 1986.

DOCUMENT 10: ARRIVING AT THE CONCENTRATION CAMPS

Dutch citizen Corrie ten Boom was a Christian woman who hid Jews during the war. When she was caught by the Nazis, she and her family were sent first to a Dutch prison, and then to Ravensbruck, a concentration camp. Here she describes what it was like when she and her sister arrived at such a forsaken place.

From the crest of the hill we saw it, like a vast scar on the green Ger-man landscape; a city of low gray barracks surrounded by concrete wails on which guard towers rose at intervals. In the very center, a square smokestack emitted a thin gray vapor into the blue sky.

"Ravensbruck!"

Like a whispered curse the word passed back through the lines. This was the notorious women's extermination camp whose name we had heard even in Haarlem. That squat concrete building, that smoke disappearing in the bright sunlight—no! I would not look at it! As Betsie and I stumbled down the hill, I felt the Bible bumping between my shoulder blades. God's good news. Was it to this world that He had spoken it?

Now we were close enough to see the skull-and-crossbones posted at intervals on the walls to warn of electrified wiring along the top. The massive iron gates swung in; we marched between them. Acres of soot-gray barracks stretched ahead of us. Just inside the wall was a row of waist-high water spigots. We charged them, thrusting hands, arms, legs, even heads, under the streams of water, washing away the stench of the boxcars. A squad of women guards in dark blue uniforms rushed at us, hauling and shouting, swinging their short, hard crops.

At last they drove us back from the faucets and herded us down an avenue between barracks. This camp appeared far grimmer than the one we had left. At least, in marches about Vught, we had caught sight of fields and woods. Here, every vista ended in the same concrete barrier; the camp was set down in a vast man-made valley rising on every side to those towering wire-topped walls.

At last we halted. In front of us a vast canvas tent-roof—no sides—covered an acre or more of straw-strewn ground. Betsie and I found a spot on the edge of this area and sank gratefully down. Instantly we were on our feet again. Lice! The straw was literally alive with them. We stood for a while, clutching blankets and pillowcases well away from the infested ground. But at last we spread our blankets over the squirming straw and sat on them.

Some of the prisoners had brought scissors from Vught: everywhere beneath the huge tent women were cutting one another's hair. A pair was passed to us. Of course we must do the same, long hair was folly in such a place. But as I cut Betsie's chestnut waves, I cried.

Toward evening there was a commotion at one end of the tent. A line of S.S. guards was moving across it, driving women out from under the canvas. We scrambled to our feet and snatched up our blankets as they bore down upon us. Perhaps a hundred yards beyond the tent the chase stopped. We stood about, uncertain what to do. Whether a new group of prisoners had arrived or what the reason was for driving us from the tent, no one knew. Women began spreading their blankets on the hard cinder ground. Slowly it dawned on Betsie and me that we were to spend the night here where we stood. We laid my blanket on the ground, stretched out side by side and pulled hers over us.

"The night is dark and I am far from home . . ." Betsie's sweet so-prano was picked up by voices all around us. "Lead Thou me on. . . .'"

We were waked up some time in the middle of the night by a clap of thunder and a deluge of rain. The blankets soaked through and water gathered in puddles beneath us. In the morning the field was a vast sodden swamp: hands, clothes, and faces were black from the cinder mud.

We were still wringing water from our blankets when the command came to line up for coffee. It was not coffee but a thin liquid of approximately the same color and we were grateful to get it as we shuffled double-file past the makeshift field kitchen. There was a slice of black bread for each prisoner too, then nothing more until we were given a ladle of turnip soup and a small boiled potato late in the afternoon.

Corrie ten Boom, *The Hiding Place*. Washington Depot, CT: Chosen Books, 1971.

DOCUMENT 11: ARRIVING AT BERGEN-BELSEN

Because Anne Frank's diary ends with her arrest, readers don't know what she experienced as she moved from prison to Bergen-Belsen concentration camp. Renee H. was, like Anne, a concentration camp inmate without her parents. Renee, however, survived to write about her experience as she arrived at Bergen-Belsen.

We arrived in Bergen-Belsen. It was at night. I remember spending the early part of the night looking out through an opening in the car, which they had opened because they didn't want people screaming. There was some screaming going on because of the tightness of the air—to let in fresh air. I remember seeing houses and just rims of light, because there was blackout and all you could see was the rims of light from some of the windows. So I knew we were in a town and I thought maybe, just by hope-against-hope, that maybe we had been sent back to Bratislava. It turned out not to be Bratislava but it was Hannover, Germany.

A little while later, we arrived in camp, and then there was a long march. The march was the most horrendous thing I have experienced because after eight days the people were just in no shape to walk from the station to the reception house at the camp, and that march seemed endless. It looked enormously long. In my mind now it seems like three hours. The Germans kept shouting and yelling. There were truncheons and dogs, and they would fall on the people. We finally arrived, and we were assigned a block. I remember thinking to myself, "I'm so exhausted. I must sleep." I remember the first night falling asleep. I had nothing to eat for a long, long time, nothing to drink. Because I wasn't in Auschwitz with my parents, and I remember saying to myself, "I will never stop looking for them." I remember thinking life had played a terrible trick on me.

Joshua M. Greene and Shiva Kumar, eds., *Witness: Voices from the Holocaust*. New York: The Free Press, 2000.

DOCUMENT 12: DUTCH COLLABORATION

While the Nazis were undeniably the force that caused the persecution and death of thousands of Jews through Europe, they were not without assistance. This short excerpt points out that the Dutch were willing to accept and even assist the Nazis in their quest to eliminate the Jews.

In the West there was no country which had such a high extermination quota as the Netherlands. Based on this statement a number of questions arise, especially in regard to the behavior of non-Jewish citizens during the persecution of the Jews.

The problem could best be illuminated by an example: Anne Frank was murdered by a German, she was arrested by an Austrian, and she was betrayed by a Dutchman. How exemplary is the case of Anne Frank for the persecution of the Jews in the Netherlands? In other words: what was the extent of the collaboration of the non-Jewish Dutch citizens with the German occupational force during the persecution of the Jews?

These persecutions were initiated and carried out by Germans under the leadership of Austrians, such as the Reich's commissioner Seyss-Inquart, the higher-ranking SS officer and police chief Rauter, and a number of top officials who almost exclusively belonged to the so-called Austrian Connection.

However, it is also a fact that after Queen Wilhelmina and her ministers left for England, the Dutch civilian administration continued to work quite loyally and also executed the Anti-Jewish measures under this German-Austrian leadership without hesitation.

In regard to this, I would like to quote the Dutch historian Ben Sijes:

The decision of the general secretaries (they were the highest officials in the administrative bureaucracy) to collaborate loyally with the Germans had far-reaching consequences. The general secretaries not only passively provided an example, but they also incited the entire officialdom, the economic life, even the Dutch society as a whole, to follow their example. The general secretaries did not offer a convincing resistance, and therefore their protest also could not impress the Germans. Without a doubt this must have led to the consequence that the Germans seized the opportunity all the more to carry out unweariedly and as quickly as possible their task which was already fulfilled in Germany and in other occupied territories. Instead of shielding the Jews, who, after all, were also citizens of the Netherlands, the general secretaries let them down. Practically, this meant that the Jews could not count on any protection from the Dutch state institutions. This situation contributed to the fact that the Jews could later be declared free as birds—and the general secretaries acted as accomplices to this.

Surely, this is a tough but, unfortunately, a generally fair assessment. The objections by the general secretaries *against* the anti-Jewish measures of the occupational power had just as little credibility as their collaboration in *carrying out* these measures. However, the result was quite satisfactory, if one viewed it from the point of view of the persecutor.

Jörg Wollenberg, ed., *The German Public and the Persecution of the Jews, 1933–1945: "No One Participated, No One Knew,"* trans. Rado Pribic. New Jersey: Humanities Press International, Inc., 1996.

DOCUMENT 13: MEIN KAMPF: HITLER'S BELIEFS

Long before he became the chancellor of Germany, Adolf Hitler was an angry young politician. In 1925 and 1926 he published Mein Kampf *(which means* "My Struggle"*), telling about his beliefs and political agenda. This excerpt is a typical example of his virulent anti-Semitism.*

The Jew's domination in the state seems so assured that now not only can he call himself a Jew again, but he ruthlessly admits his ultimate national and political designs. A section of his race openly owns itself to be a foreign people, yet even here they lie. For while the Zionists (Jews who want to create their own state) try to make the rest of the world believe that the national consciousness of the Jew finds its satisfaction in the creation of a Palestinian state, the Jews again slyly dupe the dumb *Goyim* (non-Jewish people). It doesn't even enter their heads to build up a Jewish state in Palestine for the purpose of living there; all they want is a central organization for their international world swindle, endowed with its own sovereign rights and removed from the intervention of other states: a haven for convicted scoundrels and a university for budding crooks.

It is a sign of their rising confidence and sense of security that at a time when one section is still playing the German, Frenchman, or Englishman, the other with open effrontery comes out as the Jewish race.

How close they see approaching victory can be seen by the hideous aspect which their relations with the members of other peoples takes on.

With satanic joy in his face, the black-haired Jewish youth lurks in wait for the unsuspecting girl whom he defiles with his blood, thus stealing her from her people. With every means he tries to destroy the racial foundations of the people he has set out to subjugate. Just as he himself systematically ruins women and girls, he does not shrink back from pulling down the blood barriers for others, even on a large scale. It was and it is Jews who bring the Negroes into the Rhineland, always with the same secret thought and clear aim of ruining the hated white race by the necessarily resulting bastardization, throwing it down from its cultural and political height, and himself rising to be its master.

For a racially pure people which is conscious of its blood can never be enslaved by the Jew. In this world he will forever be master over bastards and bastards alone.

And so he tries systematically to lower the racial level by a continuous poisoning of individuals.

And in politics he begins to replace the idea of democracy by the dictatorship of the proletariat.

In the organized mass of Marxism he has found the weapon which lets him dispense with democracy and in its stead allows him to subjugate and govern the peoples with a dictatorial and brutal fist.

He works systematically for revolutionization in a twofold sense: economic and political.

Around peoples who offer too violent a resistance to attack from within he weaves a net of enemies, thanks to his international influence, incites them to war, and finally, if necessary, plants a flag of revolution on the very battlefields.

In economics he undermines the states until the social enterprises which have become unprofitable are taken from the state and subjected to his financial control.

In the political field he refuses the state the means for its self-preservation, destroys the foundations of all national self-maintenance and defense, destroys faith in the leadership, scoffs at its history and past, and drags everything that is truly great into the gutter.

Adolf Hitler, *Mein Kampf*, trans. Ralph Manheim. New York: Houghton Mifflin, 1969.

DOCUMENT 14: THE NUREMBERG LAWS

By 1935, the German government began to create laws further restricting the Jews' ability to live as citizens in Germany, and eventually in all of the Nazi-occupied countries, including Holland. The most well-known of these laws were called the Nuremberg Laws because they were first announced at a rally in the city of Nuremberg, Germany.

September 15, 1935

Law for the Protection of German Blood and German Honor

"Marriages between Jews and subjects of German or kindred blood are forbidden . . . Extramarital intercourse forbidden between Jews and subjects of German or kindred blood . . . Jews are forbidden to fly the Reich and national flag and to display Reich colors . . . They are, on the other hand, allowed to display the Jewish colors . . . Whoever violates the prohibition . . . will be punished by penal servitude."

September 15, 1935

Reich Citizenship Law

"A Reich citizen is only that subject of German or kindred blood who proves by his conduct that he is willing and suited loyally to serve the German people and the Reich."

November 14, 1935

First Decree to the Reich Citizenship Law

"A Jew cannot be a Reich citizen. He is not entitled to the right to vote on political matters: he cannot hold public office . . . A Jew is anyone descended from at least three grandparents who are fully Jewish as regards race . . . Also deemed a Jew is a Jewish Mischlung subject who is descended from two fully Jewish grandparents and . . . who belonged to the Jewish religious community . . . who was married to a Jew . . . who is the offspring of a marriage concluded by a Jew . . . who is an offspring of extramarital intercourse with a Jew . . ."

August 17, 1938
Second Decree for the Implementation of the Law Regarding Changes of Family Names
"Jews may be given only such given names as are listed in the Guidelines on the Use of Given Names issued by the Reich Minister of the Interior . . . Insofar as Jews have other given names than those which may be given to Jews . . . they are obligated, beginning January 1, 1939, to assume an additional given name, namely the given name Israel in the case of males and the given name Sarah in the case of females."

Nuremberg Laws, 1935, 1938.

DOCUMENT 15: NAZI VIEWS ON THE SOLUTION TO THE JEWISH QUESTION

This document from a Nazi publication of 1938 clearly shows the twisted rationale behind the Nazi laws, which began by simple persecution but ultimately led to the mass murder of the Jewish people.

There is a view that is heard at every step: if we had solved the Jewish Question completely and by the most brutal methods back in 1933, the outcry would have been no worse than it has been all the time since then, because we are solving the Jewish Question piecemeal, by single measures forced on us by the Jews themselves and their friends. This view is correct in itself. But it had to remain theoretical because at that time we lacked the *military might that we possess today.* At that time the Jews might have succeeded in inciting the nations into a war of revenge against us; today the loudest of the democratic screechers will be the ones to hesitate the longest.

Because it is necessary, because we no longer hear the worlds screaming, and finally because no power in the world can stop us, we shall therefore now take the Jewish Question towards its final solution. The program is clear.

It is: total elimination, complete separation!

What does that mean?

It means *not only* the elimination of the Jews from the German national economy, a position which they brought upon themselves following their murderous attack and their incitement to war and murder.

It means much more!

It can no longer be asked of any German that he should continue to live under one roof with Jews, a race stamped with the mark of murderers and criminals, and deadly enemies of the German people.

The Jews must therefore be driven out of our apartment houses and residential areas and put into series of streets or blocks of houses where they will be together and have as little contact as possible with Germans. They must be marked and the right must be taken from them to own houses or land or a share in either, because it cannot be expected of a German that he should submit to the power of a Jewish landlord and maintain him by the work of his hands.

Das Schwarze Korps, No. 47, November 24, 1938.

Chronology

May 12, 1889
Anne's father, Otto Frank, is born in Germany.

January 16, 1900
Anne's mother, Edith Hollander, is born in Germany.

1914–1918
World War I.

April 1, 1920
Adolf Hitler joins the Nationalist Socialist German Workers' Party (the Nazi Party).

January 1923
The Nazi Party holds its first rally.

May 12, 1925
Anne's parents are married in Aachen, Germany.

February 16, 1926
Anne's older sister, Margot, is born in Germany.

June 12, 1929
Anneliese Marie (known as Anne) is born in Germany.

July 31, 1932
The Nazi Party forms a coalition government in Germany.

January 30, 1933
Hitler is appointed chancellor of Germany.

Spring 1933
The Nazi Party suspends freedom of speech; the Gestapo, the

state-run secret police, is established; the first concentration camp, Dachau, is built as a means to house political prisoners; the Nazi Party boycotts many Jewish businesses; Jews are not allowed to teach or hold public office; Otto Frank begins to plan for his family to flee Germany.

SEPTEMBER 1933

Otto Frank moves to Amsterdam, Holland, and sets up his new business.

DECEMBER 1933

Edith and Margot Frank join Otto in Amsterdam.

FEBRUARY 1934

Anne moves to Amsterdam.

1934

Anne attends the Montessori kindergarten.

1934–1938

The Nazi Party continues to persecute Jews and begins to plan for the takeover of Europe, beginning with Austria.

SUMMER 1937

The van Pels family also leaves Germany for Holland.

NOVEMBER 9–10, 1938

In Germany and Austria, the state sponsors the destruction of Jewish businesses and synagogues. The event is called *Kristallnacht* or the "Night of Broken Glass" from the many shattered store windows.

DECEMBER 8, 1938

Fritz Pfeffer leaves Germany and emigrates to Holland.

SEPTEMBER 1, 1939

Hitler invades Poland. World War II begins.

APRIL–MAY 1940

Germany successfully invades Denmark, Norway, France, Belgium, Luxembourg, and the Netherlands.

MAY 8, 1941

Otto Frank changes the name and ownership of his company so that it is no longer considered a Jewish business.

SUMMER 1941

By Nazi order, Anne and Margot must leave their schools to attend an all-Jewish school in Amsterdam.

DECEMBER 11, 1941

Germany declares war on the United States.

SPRING 1942

The main concentration camps of Sobibor, Belzec, Treblinka, and Auschwitz-Birkenau become fully operational as death camps.

JUNE 12, 1942

Anne turns thirteen. She receives a diary for her birthday.

JULY 5, 1942

Margot receives a call-up notice to leave for a work camp.

JULY 6, 1942

The entire Frank family goes into hiding in the "Secret Annex" at 263 Prinsengracht, the address of Otto's offices.

JULY 13, 1942

The van Pels family enters the Secret Annex.

NOVEMBER 16, 1942

Fritz Pfeffer enters the annex.

AUGUST 4, 1944

The Secret Annex is discovered. All eight residents are arrested and taken to the police station. Soon they are transferred to Westerbork transit camp in Holland.

SEPTEMBER 3, 1944

All eight residents are transferred, via cattle car, to Auschwitz concentration camp in Poland.

SEPTEMBER 6, 1944

Hermann van Pels is gassed at Auschwitz.

OCTOBER 6, 1944

Anne and Margot Frank are transferred from Auschwitz to Bergen-Belsen concentration camp in Germany.

NOVEMBER 1944

High officials in the Nazi Party, recognizing that the Germans are about to lose the war, order the crematoria in concentration camps to be destroyed.

DECEMBER 20, 1944

Fritz Pfeffer dies in Neuengamme concentration camp.

JANUARY 6, 1945

Edith Hollander Frank dies at Auschwitz.

JANUARY 27, 1945

The Russian army liberates Auschwitz. Otto Frank is among the survivors.

FEBRUARY OR MARCH 1945

Anne and Margot die within days of each other at Bergen-Belsen, probably of typhus.

APRIL 30, 1945

Adolf Hitler commits suicide.

MAY 1945

Peter van Pels dies in Mauthausen concentration camp.

MAY 7, 1945

Germany surrenders, ending the war in Europe.

SPRING 1945

Auguste van Pels dies in Theresienstadt concentration camp.

JUNE 1945

Otto Frank returns to Amsterdam.

OCTOBER 1945

Otto Frank learns that Anne and Margot died in Bergen-Belsen.

SPRING 1946

An article in a Dutch journal mentions Anne's diary.

SUMMER 1947

Anne's diary is published in Amsterdam.

1951

The diary is translated into English.

AUGUST 19, 1980

Otto Frank, the only resident of the annex to survive the war, dies in Switzerland.

FOR FURTHER RESEARCH

THE WRITINGS OF ANNE FRANK

Anne Frank, *Anne Frank's Tales from the Secret Annex.* Trans. Ralph Manheim and Michel Mok. Previously published in part as *Tales from the House Behind.* New York: Bantam Books, 1994.

Anne Frank, *Anne Frank: The Diary of a Young Girl.* Trans. B.M. Mooyaart—Doubleday. New York: Pocket Books, 1972.

Anne Frank, *The Diary of Anne Frank: The Critical Edition.* Ed. David Barnouw and Gerrold van der Stroom. Trans. Arnold J. Pomerans and B.M. Mooyaart—Doubleday. New York: Doubleday, 1989.

Anne Frank, *The Diary of a Young Girl: The Definitive Edition.* Ed. Otto H. Frank and Mirjam Pressler. Trans. Susan Massotty. London: Penguin, 1997.

BIOGRAPHICAL WORKS ABOUT ANNE FRANK

Miep Gies and Alison Leslie Gold, *Anne Frank Remembered: The Story of the Woman Who Helped to Hide the Frank Family.* New York: Simon & Schuster, 1987.

Alison Leslie Gold, *Memories of Anne Frank: Reflections of a Childhood Friend.* New York: Scholastic Press, 1997.

Frances Goodrich and Albert Hackett, *The Diary of Anne Frank: A Random House Play.* Based on trans. by B.M. Mooyaart—Doubleday. New York: Random House, 1955.

Hedda Rosner Kopf, *Understanding Anne Frank's* The Diary of a Young Girl. Westport, CT: Greenwood Press, 1997.

Willy Lindwer, *The Last Seven Months of Anne Frank.* Trans. Alison Meersschaert. New York: Pantheon Books, 1991.

Melissa Müller, *Anne Frank: The Biography.* Trans. Rita and

Robert Kimber. New York: Henry Holt and Company, 1998.

Mirjam Pressler, *Anne Frank: A Hidden Life.* Trans. Anthea Bell. New York: Dutton Children's Books, 1999.

Ernst Schnabel, *Anne Frank: A Portrait in Courage.* Trans. Richard Winston and Clara Winston. New York: Harcourt, Brace, 1958.

Ruud van der Rol and Rian Verhoeven, *Beyond the Diary: Photographic Remembrance.* Trans. Tony Lanham and Plym Peters. New York: Viking Press, 1993.

HISTORICAL WORKS

Susan Bachrach, *Tell Them We Remember: The Story of the Holocaust.* Boston: Little, Brown, 1994.

Jacob Boas, ed., *We Are Witnesses: Five Diaries of Teenagers Who Died in the Holocaust.* New York: Henry Holt, 1995.

Eva Schloss, *Eva's Story: A Survivor's Tale.* New York: St. Martin's Press, 1988.

Corrie ten Boom, *The Hiding Place.* Washington Depot, CT: Chosen Books, 1971.

WEBSITES

The Anne Frank Center USA, www.annefrank.com. This site has an amazing array of materials, including media resources, chronology, exhibitions, teacher and student resource material, and a bookstore.

The ANNE FRANK-Fonds (Foundation), www.annefrank. ch/e/. Located in Basle, Switzerland, this organization is dedicated to the promotion of the values that Anne Frank exhibited. Basic information about Anne, her diary, and the foundation itself are available in English, Spanish, and German.

The Anne Frank House, www.annefrank.nl. Although this is a Dutch site, there is an English link which provides access to information about the "Secret Annex," as well as many links and resources for learning more about Anne Frank.

The Anne Frank Internet Guide, www-th.phys.rug.nl/~ma/ annefrank.html#. This is a personal, unsponsored website, and provides information and links to information about Anne Frank found throughout the world wide web.

The Anne Frank Trust, UK, www.afet.org.uk. Formed in 1991 as a sister site to the Anne Frank House. Like its American counterpart (The Anne Frank Center USA), this British website provides information about Anne Frank and her life, study resources, bibliographies, and many photos.

INDEX